Port Isaac, Port Quin, Pendoggett, Port Gaverne and Trelights.

Volume Three

Port Isaac at Play and at Prayer

By

Geoff Provis

Published by Trefreock Publications

First published December 2013.

© Copyright Geoff Provis 2013.

No part of this publication may be reproduced without permission
of the publisher.

Published by Trefreock Publications,
18 Highfield Park Road,
Launceston Cornwall PL15 7DY.
01566 775820

ISBN 978-0-9562998-2-6

Cover design by Geoff Provis.

Front cover top: Local men 'yarn' at Port Isaac Harbour.
A scene rather taken for granted until it disappeared following the ever increasing tide of holiday homes.
From the left: Trevor Platt, (Trevor helped John Glover fish in his boat the Swift); John Glover, Norman 'Ningy'
Short and his brother Charlie Short; Tommy Tabb, Jim Provis and his brother Anthony 'Antny' Provis the harbourmaster.
The photographer was Ann Smith, a regular visitor to Port Isaac, and a friend of Tom Saundry, John Glover and Norman Short.
This is no doubt why the men appear to be posing for the photo which was very unusual.
Courtesy of Ann Smith. C 1960.
Lower left: A Band of Hope parade makes its way slowly up Fore Street, Port Isaac.
Courtesy of Stephen Found.
Lower right: John Wesley, the founder of Methodism who visited Port Isaac on a
number of occasions during the eighteenth century.
NPG317 John Wesley by William Hamilton, oil on canvas, 1788. Credit line © National Portrait Gallery.
The cover is red, the colour of the long defunct Port Isaac Old Cornwall Society.

Printed by Booths Print
The Praze, Penryn, Cornwall, TR10 8AA
01326 373628

Contents.

Introduction.

This, the third book in my series of life at Port Isaac, Port Gaverne, Port Quin, includes the small villages of Trelights and Pendoggett. It deals with the way the local population socialized, played games, and prayed together up until about 1970. For many years the population of Port Isaac was about one thousand, whereas the populations of neighbouring hamlets and villages were relatively small. When I describe the various activities, the reader must appreciate that there was no mass communication which is available today, so people made their own entertainment, games and social interaction. Attendances at churches and chapels were high in comparison with today, and many activities were associated with these religions. Is it the case therefore, that as societies become more affluent, religious dedication decreases?

In 1895, the Methodist Chapels in the area around Port Isaac boasted two choirs at Port Isaac, and single choirs at Trelights, Pendoggett, Trelill, St Mabyn, St Tudy, St Teath, Camelford, Boscastle, De Lank, Tredrizzick and Wadebridge. As well as this, the chapels played a major role in the social life of the villages and small towns of North Cornwall, and I explore this relationship. I do not deal with the history of Methodism in the Port Isaac area, but hopefully I include sufficient to enable the reader to appreciate the role the chapels played in social life in previous days.

Sunday was the day of rest, but many people did not go out because they could not afford 'Sunday', or best clothes. Children shared shoes and clothes, and families were huddled together in tiny cottages, but this same hardship helped forge a close community spirit which cannot be matched today. The very character of the local people was forged by their living conditions, so I ask the reader to appreciate this whilst reading this volume.

As the traditional industries of Port Isaac died out such as the export of corn, slate, pilchard, herring, and the sailing ship trade; numerous men of the port were forced to seek their fortunes elsewhere, and at a later date, I count myself among their number. I recently met Henry Scorey, 93 years of age at Camborne. Henry, the son of a Port Isaac Coastguard, went to live at Port Isaac with his family when he was 12. He married Mavis Williams of the Trethowey Hotel, but in 1940 at the age of 20 he left Port Isaac, but to my amazement, he genuinely still considered Port Isaac to be his home. He talked to me movingly about how in recent years, he was driven down over Trewetha Hill and on seeing the sea, he thought he was back home. On his living room wall was a painting of Port Isaac, and I asked Henry what life was like at Port Isaac during the 1930s.

He said, "Life was wonderful, all the social activities you wanted to take part in, and summer time swims out to Gut." Gut is the narrow gap between the Main and Castle Rock at Port Gaverne.

Henry also said there were fairs, circuses, youth clubs, choirs, chapels, boxing at the Church Rooms, pulling punts in the harbour, games at school and in the village streets, dances and much singing at the chapels and the Temperance Hall. Perhaps I should add that Henry's father was a coastguard, and therefore in permanent work, so possibly some of the poorer inhabitants may have held a slightly different view to Henry. However, what is it that made Henry Scorey so loyal to Port Isaac after all these years? Why do the majority of people who were very poor look back on their youth at Port Isaac with such affection? They all agree that the village is just not the same, and has lost its very soul, and yet the people living there now are so much better off financially. In this book I describe the varied activities which the locals shared, and I hope you understand at the conclusion, that whilst poverty is very difficult to live through, it does generate a unique kind of social cohesion.

John Wesley, surely a great man, visited Port Isaac on a number of occasions, and many similar isolated communities in the mid eighteenth century, and succeeded in converting many to Christianity where most men would have failed. The fiercely parochial, stubborn Cornish were prepared to accept the message of the Gospel from this man.

Please note it was necessary to make many references to the 'Temperance Hall' in this book, as it was named as such in 1895 when it was built by and for the Band of Hope. However, for the information of visitors to Port Isaac, in recent years the name was changed to the 'Village Hall', thereby losing its historical very descriptive name.

Snobbery existed at Port Isaac as in other places, but I do not deal with this directly. To conclude my introduction, I sadly learned that Henry Scorey died just nine days after I met him at his Camborne home. I met him only once previously at a funeral at St Endellion, and then only briefly. It was a privilege to know him, if only for a brief period.

I deal with St Endellion and St Peter's Anglican Churches in a later book, although St Peter's Youth Club is included.

Geoff Provis.
2013.

Port Isaac- Games at School, Beach and Village.

The Beach.

The beach was our playground, and what a fantastic playground it proved to be. The older men, especially my grandfather, warned us of the dangers of 'ground sea', and if these were the conditions, we had to find somewhere else to play. The only 'in house' entertainment was the wireless, so we just made our own fun, and most of it was in the fresh air.

Without question, Port Gaverne Beach was much cleaner, but Port Isaac lads mainly stayed loyal to their beach, although swimming was much better at Port Gaverne. I have already explained that all the waste from cottages went into the Port Isaac Lake which ended on the beach. In addition, Port Isaac women regularly walked down Fore Street carrying a bucket of 'slops' in one hand, and a bucket of ashes in the other. All this was thrown in the chute situated at 'Little Hill', and this simply dropped straight onto the beach. The chute was just below the 'half tide' mark, so some of the waste was taken out to sea on the ebb tide. Locals who were fortunate enough to have gardens, dug a pit, and this pit took all their human waste, and it lasted for about a month before another pit was dug.

The best pump water was that at Middle Street, formerly Chapel Street, and it was always colder than the water from the pump at Mine Pit Corner; the pump outside St Peter's Church.

Chasing Rats With Dogs.

One of the earliest games or entertainments enjoyed by all ages, was 'chasing rats with dogs' on Port Isaac Beach. Briefly, rats were caught on premises in the village in small cages, and then taken onto the beach when the tide was at 'half tide'. By 'half tide', I mean that the tide was half way in, or half way up the beach. The people with the caged rats stood by the water, and the rest of the villagers formed a solid line at the top of the beach, some with their dogs. One rat at a time was released, and as the tide was half way in, the rat could not escape down the beach, and with the line of people blocking the top of the beach, escape via that route was also prevented. The high sides of the harbour prevented the rat escaping there, so the dogs then chased and killed the rat, much to the amusement of the locals who no doubt had a grandstand view from Roscarrock Hill, the Pentus, Little Hill, and also of course from the line preventing the rat escaping. I am indebted to the late Joe Saundry for this piece of information.

I am quite sure that the majority of my readers are horrified at the thought of this practice, but surely this provided some sport and excitement for the hard pressed locals. I am afraid the rats were plentiful at Port Isaac, encouraged by the lack of a sewerage system, crowded living conditions, poor storage of food, and at times, waste material from tons of herring and pilchard when in season.

Horse Racing or 'Oss Racin'.

At the times of fairs such as 'Ollacome' Fair, the locals entertained themselves in various ways. The late Joe Saundry kindly loaned me the photograph of four or five horses racing from the low water mark on Port Isaac Beach sometime before the building of the breakwaters. It is not suggested that this was serious horse racing, but possibly locals racing for money or a bet. I estimate it was taken around the turn of the twentieth century or before. I find this particular photo fascinating.

Horse racing on Port Isaac beach around about 1900, involving four or five horses. Joe Saundry said that this occurred during one of the fairs which regularly visited Port Isaac, quite possibly Holycome or 'Ollacombe' Fair. Note the small child in the foreground dressed all in white. A fascinating photo, and one which I think is quite unique. The rocks in the foreground appear to be ones on which the Western Breakwater was later built.
Courtesy of Joe Saundry.   C 1900.

Tin Can Tommy.

Our favourite place for this was the old mooring post below the Golden Lion pub. It was situated at the top of the beach just before the footpath to the cellars below the Pentus. An old tin can such as a small bean can, was half filled with stones and the top bent in by hammering it with a beach stone so that the small stones were confined in the can, and when it was shaken the can rattled. One person was 'it'. Somebody from the rest of the gang threw the can down onto the beach, and the person who was 'it' walked towards the can, picked it up and walked backwards to the mooring post so that he could not see the direction in which the others were running away to hide.

When he reached the post, he turned around to face the buildings, and he had to keep a look out for the others who were hiding. If he saw any of them, he had to shout the name of them and 'one, two, three'. At the same time as saying 'one, two, three', he had to hit the can on the post three times.

The object of the rest of the gang was to rush at the person with the can, and get it off of him before he had the chance to go through the procedure of saying everyone's name plus 'one two three'. Usually the person was wrestled to the ground, and the can forcibly removed from him. If the person holding the can failed to say the names and count 'one two three' each time, he had to have the can again, and the whole procedure was repeated. The game was invariably very rough and bruises were common place. Paul Oliver once walked back home to The Terrace sporting a black eye.

Weasel.

This game was possibly unique to Port Isaac, as I have not heard of it from any other source. I played this regularly on the beach, but nowhere else. Briefly the game consisted of two teams of ten boys, or any number to make equal teams. The game was always played against the wall below the 'Pentus', and the 'weasel' consisted of just three pieces of stick or wood picked up off the beach, and each about six to eight inches long and quite narrow. One team, the 'out' team formed a weasel by placing two pieces of wood against the wall, and the third piece was then balanced on top of the other two thus forming the weasel.

To start the game the 'weasel' was made, and a member of the 'out' team threw a ball at a member of the 'in' team who were batting. The bat usually consisted of a piece of wreck wood or anything suitable found lying on the beach. The batter stood about four or five yards in front of the boy with the ball and in front of the weasel, and the ball was thrown in any fashion at the batter. The object was to hit the ball far enough around the beach to enable the batter to run around a circular course and return to the area where the weasel was and claim one weasel. The 'out' team's job was to recover the ball and throw it back towards their player nearer the weasel, and if he caught the ball he then promptly threw it at the weasel, hopefully before the batter had returned and knock it over. If he succeeded he shouted 'weasel', and the batter was out. The batter was also out if he was hit below the waist by the ball whilst running around the course. If they were hit then that person was out of the game but the other members of the team could continue and take their turn with the bat. If all ten were hit by the ball then the game was over as the 'out' team had failed to make a weasel. If the 'out' team managed to make a weasel without being hit, then they would shout 'weasel' loudly, and the object was to count the number of weasels made. The winner was the team with the most weasels.

I have an unproven theory that this game may have been brought to Port Isaac by men returning from yachting from various parts of the world. Perhaps they saw native children playing it somewhere.

'Skimming' Slate Stones.

For very many years, builders deposited waste material on the beach, and this included broken and un-wanted slates. Also, natural slate was broken down on the beach by the waves, and these slates were ideally shaped for throwing in a flat fashion onto the surface of the sea where they skimmed the surface before finally sinking. I recall doing this regularly as a boy. Boys threw stones alongside each other to see who could skim the furthest. The smaller slates skimmed the furthest, but the largest ones skimmed in a slower fashion, and the boys sometimes counted the number of bounces the stone made before it sank.

Stone Throwing.

Some boys threw stones from the top of the beach towards the western side whilst the tide was in to see who could throw the furthest, whilst being careful not to throw any near the moored boats in the centre of the harbour. If they did so, there were always fishermen around to 'tell off' the boys.

Some boys were better than others. Peter Rowe remembers being able to reach the store pools - 'Long Pool', whilst his older brother Jack, threw to just inside the breakwater, whilst Charlie Rowe Snr was able to hit the breakwater.

Moling and Crabbing.

Local boys messing around in the rock pools either moling or crabbing. The boys at the back appear to be holding small lines with baited pins on the end trying to catch 'moles' or gobies. The other boys are probably looking for crabs beneath the pots or stones.
From the left: Steven Van Evelingen, Paul Van Evelingen, (mother Margaret Ann Glover); Alan Jahn and Steve Jahn. (mother Joan Murray).
The boat on the left is the MCB, named after Mary, Charles and Bruce; a 'Rowe' boat. The larger boat in front is the Winifred a 'Brown' boat, named after Winifred Brown, and the boat on the right is the Gleaner, a 'Provis' boat. The fisherman beyond the MCB and mooring his boat appears to be Mark Townsend. (Photo taken by a visitor).
Courtesy of Janet Chadband nee May and Joan Murray nee Honey. C1968.

Small fish named gobies, local name moles, were and still are common in the rock pools of the harbour. A favourite past-time of Port Isaac boys was catching them using a bent pin as a hook, and some cotton or thread as the line. Limpets were knocked off of rocks, and all parts of their bodies used as bait. The baited pin was simply thrown into the pool outside of an over-hanging rock, and the moles found the limpets irresistible, but once caught they were usually thrown straight back.

Finding crabs at low water beneath large stones, or getting larger crabs out of holes using wire was also popular.

Paddlers.

Every local family were aware that sea water ruins footwear, as after being soaked with sea water, a white rim appears on leather which is difficult to remove. The local lads kept a pair of shoes or sandals just for paddling or playing around in the harbour. Many referred to these as 'paddlers'.

Fish Barrels on the Platt.

Barrels stacked on the Platt awaiting the catch of herring were irresistible to the local boys, and they were expert at finding ways of climbing on and hiding in them.

Terry Thomas playing amongst the lobster pots on the Town Platt, Port Isaac. Terry was the son of Sammy Dyer Thomas, a fisherman. Previously, playing and hiding in the empty fish barrels used for the herring was even more popular.
Courtesy of Clarence Smith   C 1943.

Sailing Tin Boats.

As a means of amusement, boys and sometimes the men, made small boats made of old tin ice cream containers, or any suitable tin container. The tin was cut into a certain shape, and then bent to form a boat shape. Usually a piece of wood in the shape of a transom was placed in the stern of the boat to retain the shape. Another piece was

Peter Rowe holding a typical tin boat most of us made for sailing or playing with in the harbour or Long Pool. See also the painting on the rear cover by Ray Provis and the little boat moored in Plaice Pool. Photo by Geoff Provis.

selected to be a thwart or seat, and this was usually nailed into place. Stones were placed in the boat as ballast, and a stick put through the thwart to act as a mast on which a sail was affixed. Sometimes old matchboxes were used as sails.

Peter Rowe recalls actually mooring these tin boats in an area known as Plaice Pool, on the western side of the beach which is uncovered at 'half tide'. String was attached to stones which acted as anchors, and the other end of the string was tied to the bows and sterns of the boats in a similar manner to the real boats moored in the harbour. If the boats survived the sea overnight, the boys were delighted.

Sailing Model Yachts at the Mill Pond.

I deal with this subject in a future book, but merely mention this, as it was another means of playing games and entertainment at Port Isaac.

Padstow Visitor's Regatta, Aquatic and Athletic Sports Day.

The Royal Cornwall Gazette of the 4th August 1898, provides interesting details of a swimming match involving Port Isaac boys at the Padstow Regatta.

'Swimming match boys:

1st. Mitchell, Port Isaac; 2nd F Thomas and 3rd Russell Couch. A special prize was awarded to Walter Mitchell. (I suspect all these names are local Port Isaac boys).

Lug sail fishing boat race:

1st *Irex,* Honey; 2nd *Eliza,* C Thomas; 3rd *Kate,* W Brown; 4th *AJA,* E Cowling'.

(Again, I believe all these were from Port Isaac).

Padstow Regatta and Aquatics and Athletics Sports Day.

Royal Cornwall Gazette 9th August 1900.

'Lug & mizzen boat race:

1st *Lilla,* Brown of Port Isaac; 2nd *May Rose,* Carter of Newquay; 3rd *Boy Jack,* Thomas of Port Isaac; 4th *Audrey,* Blake of Port Isaac; 5th *Eliza,* Thomas of Port Isaac'.

On the 5th June 1900, another such race was held at Padstow Regatta between the *Audrey, May Rose* and *Eliza.* The result was as follows:-

'1st   *Audrey,*   Blake - Port Isaac - 1 hour 35 minutes - £3.

2nd   *May Rose,*   Carter - Newquay - 1 hour 36 minutes - £2.

3rd   *Eliza,*   Thomas - Port Isaac - 1 hour 38 minutes - £1.

The Newquay boat led on the first round and with the others close up. The *Audrey* then assumed the lead and won a good race by one minute'.

Although times were hard at Port Isaac, the men took time off to sail to Padstow for these sporting events.

Games Played Around the Village.

With no computer games or television, we had to make our own fun. This allied to the fact that Health & Safety had not been invented, ensured that most games played both in the school and outside it were robust and healthy, in marked contrast to many computer based activities today.

Cornish 'Wrasslin'. (Wrestling).

This was a very popular sport, and many villages in North Cornwall held wrestling tournaments. These continued up until World War Two, and at Port Isaac tournaments were held in a field at Short Lane. The emphasis was on entertainment, and at the lower end of the field there were stalls selling various items, including stalls where games were played in a similar fashion to fair ground games. Some traders brought their horses and wagons to Port Isaac just for the event, and one of those was Mr Marwood Commins of Delabole who sold 'home made' sweets, and Mr Kinsman of Bodmin. Port Isaac produced some very good wrestlers; John Glover, who was a Cornish champion and someone I knew well; Andrew Mitchell, Norman Short, Bill Saundry and Tom Saundry to name but a few. Tom injured his back wrestling, and from that time on he had to wear a special corset.

John Glover of Port Isaac takes on his opponent at St Kew. The referee on the right is known as a 'stick-ler'. Note the good sized crowd. These events occurred opposite the pub at St Kew. John was the middle weight champion of Cornwall. John's family say that he is the lighter wrestler, probably the one on the left. Courtesy of Cornwall County Record Office. C 1930.

Norman Short, nicknames, 'Chingy' or 'Gurnin', taught Trevan and Edmund Hamley to wrestle.

A newspaper report dated 5th September 1927 gives details of the Cornish Championships at Newquay when John Glover retained his title:

'The finals of the Great Britain championship belts in the Cornish style of wrestling were held at Newquay on Saturday, when some thousands of enthusiasts witnessed the best and most closely contested events for many years. There were five championships, the holders defending their titles against challengers who had been chosen through eliminating contests in which some London entrants were defeated.

John Glover in later years holding a white conger on Port Isaac beach which he probably found inside one of his lobster pots. Note his strong arms, no doubt honed by his wrestling exploits and years of hauling pots single handedly. Courtesy of Ann Smith - a visitor to Port Isaac. C 1965.

Most of the bouts were of prolonged character, and that of the feather-weight occupying, with intervals for rest, about two hours, whilst the chief event for the heavy-weights provided a fine struggle for fifty minutes. Each championship was decided by the best two of three falls. John Glover of Port Isaac retained his title as middle-weight champion by securing two falls over H Gregory, Mawgan'.

An interesting quote which shows the popularity and arduous nature of this Cornish sport

Clarence Smith recalls that women wrestled at Ollacombe Fair, and that another Port Isaac man who shall remain nameless, accidentally killed an opponent during a bout at St Kew, and he never wrestled again.

Sam Bunt and Andrew Mitchell also were sticklers, which is another word for a referee.

Sometimes the local youths wrestled each other in a friendly manner in the village. George May recalled wrestling with Vernon Lobb and Tommy Chapman, when Tommy lost his temper and kicked chips out of the Lifeboat House wall.

Big crowds were the norm at these wrestling tournaments, and although entry was free, a collection was made during the event. Spectators sometimes bet small amounts with each other on the outcome of the matches.

The Port Isaac tournament was held yearly, and a good crowd was ensured, boosted by visiting supporters from surrounding villages. Local boys were enthusiastic supporters of their fellow villagers.

The following is a quote from the Cornishman Newspaper dated 16th August 1906: 'Port Isaac's annual wrestling matches took place on Saturday in a field at Short Lane. There was a large attendance, and some very good sport was shown. There were sixteen entries, some of the competitors coming from Plymouth'.

Len Harvey the famous Cornish born boxing champion, (born 11th July 1907 at Stoke Climsland), was a special guest at one tournament at Short Lane, and he was a hero to Bob Prout. Bob shook Len's hand, and he nearly had it crushed, such was Len Harvey's grip.

Most wrestling stopped before the Second World War. The locals always pronounced wrestling as 'wrasslin'.

Cornish wrestling differs from normal wrestling as the opponents wear a cloth jacket which they take hold of and try to unbalance each other. There are various moves to put their opponent on the ground and when this is achieved the bout is over. It is part of Cornish culture and history, and although it is only now practiced by a few, it is hoped this centuries old sport, probably the oldest in the British Isles, may be resurrected. It is a very 'sporting' affair, and after each fall, the opponents shake hands as well as at the beginning and end of each bout.

Girls Jumping on the back of Empty Horse Carriages.

Anita Bunt nee Couch remembers Prout's horse drawn carriages arriving back from Port Isaac Road Station empty, and young girls taking advantage by jumping on the step at the back of the carriage, and holding on whilst it slowly made its way through the village.

Prison Bars

This game was played by two teams which comprised any number. It took place near the Town Platt, and there were four points as follows:

A line was drawn with chalk from the corner of the Lifeboat House nearest Middle Street straight across the road to the Platt. Another line was drawn from the other corner of the Lifeboat House to the Platt, but this time at a slight angle. This effectively made a square, and a further line was drawn along the centre of the square in the same direction as the road. The two teams stood in each section of the square.

Teams were picked by the team leaders, and to decide who had first pick, a slate stone was picked up from the beach, and one side was spat on. The stone was then thrown in the air, and one of the team captains shouted 'wet' or 'dry'. If the slate landed 'wet side' up then the team picked first if their captain guessed that way.

The game started when one player from a team ran off up Church Hill for a short distance being chased by a member of the other team. The person had to run around either Hawken's Bridge or the turning a little further up by the butchers, and then down Middle Street to re-join his team. If he was touched he was out of the game, and if he was not touched he re-joined his mates back in the 'prison' or 'den'. The winner was the team with most players in the 'prison' or 'den'.

Billy 'Pom Pom' Brown Jnr informed me that he played the game in a slightly different manner as follows:

A Square was drawn in front of the new Lifeboat House which was the prison. Another square was drawn opposite the Lifeboat House on the harbour side. Both teams occupied their respective squares. The object for members of the team on the harbour side was to reach an old cast iron round water hydrant situated in front of the Slipway House and not far from the Lifeboat House. If they were touched by the 'prison' team before they reached the hydrant then they ended up in the prison, and they then became one of their opponents. If they reached the hydrant without being touched, they then had to run around the block as described above with the object of returning to their original square without being touched. Much distraction was used to 'put off' opponents before attempting to run around the course.

Playing in old Abandoned Cottages.

At the turn of the twentieth century, the lower portion of Port Isaac was condemned, and the expectation was that it would be knocked down. Youngsters happily made full use of these properties by using them for the various forms of 'hide and seek'.

Members of the Thomas, Glover and Smith families, playing in an old derelict car in the Manor House, Port Isaac. The Prout family owned this house at the time.
Boys from the left: Clarence Smith, Stanley Smith, (their mother was a Glover) and Raymond Glover.
Girls from the left: A Thomas girl; a Thomas girl; Lilian Thomas, Margaret Ann Glover and Jean Thomas.
The girl in front of them facing the camera is Amanda Burnard nee Kent.
A super photo showing the children making the most of their surroundings.
Courtesy of Clarence Smith.   C 1925.

Five Stones or 'Dabbs'.

This was often played on the Town Platt or in a quiet street. Five small stones were selected which were small enough to hold in one hand. The five stones were then thrown onto the ground, and the player then picked up one stone and threw it into the air. Before this stone fell to the ground he had to pick up another stone in his hand and catch the stone previously thrown. The next time the player again threw a stone into the air whilst still holding onto the stone he had previously caught. This time he had to pick up a second stone and hold it in his hand and catch the falling stone. This continued until all stones had been picked up.

If a player dropped a stone, then he had to 'pass', and the next player had a go until all five stones were held by a player.

Clodgetts.

In the game named 'clodgetts', there were two teams, and one team ran off around the village. A favourite area was Roscarrock Hill, and then if it was fine weather, occasionally out to Lobber and Pinehoun, but usually it was in the village. (Note, Pine Haven is the name used in recent times. However, Cornish for Haven is 'Hean', and when I grew up in Port Isaac, the name was pronounced as Pine 'Hawn' or 'Houn'). A team, usually consisting of two, ran off, hid away and shouted 'clodgetts'. If the searching team came too close to the other team, the people hiding ran off again, and again hid. Once they were found, the game was over. If the team ran off into the village, they hid on roof tops, and certain buildings were ideal for this, such as the Liberal Club, the old chemist shop which is now 60 Fore Street, and directly opposite the old school, and the cottages opposite 1 Rose Hill. Jack Couch and Joe Saundry regularly hid in the stables in Trewetha Lane opposite the Temperance Hall after shouting, as they were very inefficient, and gales regularly put them out. These stables have now been converted into a dwelling. The dark narrow alleyways and 'opes' of the old village made ideal hiding places. Therefore this was mainly played in the village during dark evenings when oil lamps lit the village.

Arrow Chase.

Jack Rowe remembered this unusual game: A boy collected a soft stone such as slate off the beach and set off around the village scratching out the shape of an arrow in the road with the stone roughly every fifty yards. The rest counted to a hundred, and then set off following the arrows, and putting a line through each arrow as they passed them. Eventually when the boy was caught, the game ended.

Looking For Cheney Hunt.

Many years ago, a family named Cheney owned Bodannon, and over the years it has been handed down that a ghost exists named 'Cheney Hunt'. I have been told that I am responsible for starting this silly game which is quite possible:

During days of horse travel when many donkeys were kept in the fields above the Methodist Chapel, boys and girls enjoyed themselves larking around with these faithful placid animals.
Courtesy of Stephen Found.   C 1900.

Occasionally on a dark quiet evening a gang of us Port Isaac boys decided that we wanted to find Cheney Hunt. This involved walking up to a field at Trewetha or to Saundry's orchard in Port Isaac Valley. Once we arrived at our destination, we remained silent until something caught our attention such as an owl screeching or some other noise of nature. Then without warning one of us shouted out, "Cheney!"

A very old photo showing the lower portion of Church Hill, and Tremaine's shop on the left. (Note the large shop sign). Two local children are playing in the street which is mainly used by horses. Another local boy is looking out the door of his home. The streets then were a major playground for the children, as well as the beaches and valleys.
Courtesy of Malcolm McCarthy.   CC 1905.

Three young children listen to two older locals talking in Church Hill while a sailing vessel slowly makes its way out of Port Isaac Harbour. The older locals kept a close eye on the children in those days, the village being a close community although there was severe poverty.
Courtesy of Malcolm McCarthy.   C 1905.

Three Port Isaac girls playing in and around a boat on its moorings in the harbour.
The two girls on the left are Yvonne Cleave nee Leverton at the back, and Bernice Leverton. Joan Murray nee Honey is on the mast.
Courtesy of Stephen Found.   C 1940.

We all then ran as fast as possible back to Port Isaac shouting "Cheney's after us."

In the case of Port Isaac Valley, this involved running past the Mill Pool, on narrow tracks past the Mill and on down to Port Isaac until we arrived thoroughly exhausted. I am pleased to relate that Cheney never caught us.

On one occasion we were in a field at Trewetha when Sam Blake caught us just standing in one of his fields waiting for Cheney.

Sam said to me, "I'm surprised at you Geoffrey." Perhaps he had a point!

Signals.

When I was a young lad we played a similar game in the village, and we named it 'signals'. It was the same as 'clodgetts', except that we made signals such as a bird call or any noise at all to assist the followers.

'Oller we Shall Folla'.

This was pronounced locally as 'oller we shall folla'.

Another similar game, and was played as follows. One person ran off into the village, and someone from the group shouted, 'Oller, we shall folla'. The person being chased then shouted something back and ran off before the chasing ones could find him. This was repeated until all were caught.

'Shinning up' Temple Bar.
(Squeeze Belly Alley).

Hermon Spry recalled living at Port Isaac during the early days of the twentieth century. He said a popular game with boys then, was to climb up the walls of Temple Bar, placing one foot on each wall until they reached the top. They then remained pinned against the ceiling of the alleyway, and waited until some gentlemen wearing

Many years ago young boys climbed up Temple Bar by forcing their feet on both walls until their heads reached the top. The famous narrow width of Temple Bar made this possible. They then stayed in that position until the unsuspecting locals walked by, and then the boys touched their hats sometimes knocking them off. On average people were shorter in those days, and perhaps this assisted the boys. Picture by Geoff Provis 2013.

hats walked through the alley, when the boys promptly removed their hats. The population of the old portion of the village was high during those times, and Temple Bar was a busy thorough fare, being a short cut from Dolphin Street to Fore Street.

Please note; the name 'Squeeze Belly Alley' was only given to Temple Bar during the 1950s.

Chasers.

This was a very popular game when I was a youngster in the 1950s. Briefly, a group of youths ran off into the old part of the village and the others waited a short while before setting off to find them. Of course, when they were found the game was over. This quite simple game was surprisingly popular.

Chasing the Lake.

The Lake running through Port Isaac was flushed at various intervals and the local boys enjoyed racing the head water down to the beach. The water was held back

by a sluice gate near Leat House, and when a sufficient 'head' of water had built, the gate was released and the water rushed down through the Lake clearing it of rubbish. The boys then ran through Middle Street and across the road hoping to beat the water to the beach. The seagulls then enjoyed a feast of all the rubbish and sewage washed onto the beach.

A sluice gate was erected across Port Isaac Lake many years ago, and this was regularly used to dam the waters in order that on being released, the waters flushed the rubbish onto the beach. In my youth it was done on Tuesdays and Thursdays, but prior to that it was done on an almost daily basis. In days before the sluice was built, the miller in Port Isaac Valley released water from the Mill Pool to flush out the Lake. Local boys sometimes raced the head waters through Middle Street and down to the beach. The structure remaining is part of a later stronger one replacing the old wooden one. The resulting rubbish washed down usually produced a feeding frenzy of seagulls on the beach.
Photo by Geoff Provis.   2013

Iron Hoops.

A popular past time with the boys was rolling iron hoops around the village and beyond, using a stick to push the hoop. Leonard Mitchell was the quickest in the village at this. Very often if the boys were at Trewetha with their hoops, they deliberately broke them, and took them to Charlie Hambly the Blacksmith who repaired them there and then. Part of the attraction was that the boys had a go on the bellows.

Another similar activity was asking for tyres off of Mark Prout, of Prout Bros Port Isaac, and the boys then rolled them to Port Isaac Road Station using sticks of about two feet in length. The boys then watched the trains before returning to Port Isaac, with Leonard Mitchell always being the first back.

'Callybash' Riding.

Graham Strout remembers searching three old quarries near Trelights with his mates for pram or push chair wheels with which to make trolleys or 'callybashes to ride through the streets. We did the same at Port Isaac, but the steep hills made the riding rather hazardous.

'Old Men'.

This was very similar to 'clodgetts', when a group of local youths aged about fifteen or sixteen, sometimes about twenty, ran off into the countryside, Pinehoun being a favourite. One person then pursued them with a stick of oarweed which is a form of seaweed mainly in the shape of a stick. When caught, you had your backside smacked with the seaweed. George Couch was well known for being very handy with the seaweed.

Effect of the Second World War.

Naturally the War affected the games children played. The evacuees were all under twelve, and many were homesick and under some stress, and the Cornish children were worried about fathers who were either away at War or who were missing. As well as the normal games, sometimes the boys ran around with their arms outstretched pretending to be fighter pilots, and the girls played at being nurses. There was quite a rivalry between the locals and the evacuees, and a lot of leg pulling.

Richard Couch said that he had a great time during the war years playing with his mates and the evacuees. Many of the men folk were away at war, but the older generation kept them in order.

Pitch and Toss.

This was played with pennies, and briefly a circle was drawn and a stick placed upright in the middle. The boys threw the pennies in the circle, and the boy with the penny nearest the stick kept the lot. During World War Two on Sunday afternoons, Ian Honey, Warwick Provis, Richard Couch, Jack 'Tuffy' Spry and Mark Prout plus others of similar age, walked to Port Gaverne to play this in the Rashleigh Cellar, especially if it was raining.

Parson Billy at the Vicarage.

During the 1930s, a vicar known to the local youngsters as 'Parson Billy' regularly allowed them to play at his very large vicarage along the Cliff Road. Simple games were played there and there was a blackboard with chalk. Tea and biscuits were always available, and many of the poor children took advantage of this. I have been told that he left the fields attached to his vicarage to be used as a play area by the local children, but I have no proof of this. This is the area covered by Port Isaac Car Park. At Christmas, he also gave one hundredweight of coal to the elderly.

Marbles.

This was very popular when I was a youngster at Port Isaac. Most lads carried half a dozen or more of small marbles plus a larger one named an 'alley'. One interesting aspect was that before any game, we had to decide whether or not the game was one where the winner keeps the marbles if he wins, 'keepers', or whether the marbles are returned after the games, 'lendsies'.

A simple game was as follows: One player throws or flicks his marble away, and after it stops, his opponent flicks his own marble towards it, and if he hits it he wins. The game continued until a marble was 'hit'.

Friendly Draughts match.

A report in the Royal Cornwall Gazette of the 29th April 1895 gives details of a fascinating draughts match at Fowey. A Mr F Honey, probably Freddie, travelled all the way to Fowey, no doubt by horse transport just for this match.

'A friendly draughts match took place at Fowey on Thursday. The contestants were Mr F Honey of Port Isaac, and Mr W Furse of Fowey. Mr Honey was no match for the local player who won easily with the score of five wins and no losses, and only one drawn game.

Games Played at Home.

'Jennie' Hills, who was born at Port Isaac in 1898 recalled as a young girl playing the following games at home during the evenings: ludo, dominoes, tiddlywinks, snakes and ladders, snap and draughts. She also sewed and practiced writing, which was checked for comments, and she was never allowed out after dark, so perhaps these pastimes were not in themselves unusual. These games have an aura of innocence, and discipline in many homes was quite strict.

Games Played at Port Isaac School.

An old picture of Port Isaac School showing the boy's playground next to a precipitous cliff. This severely restricted the type of games played by us. The girls' playground was on the other side of the school and is visible from Fore Street. It was small in comparison, with none of the views of the harbour associated with the boys' area.
Provis family picture.   C 1930.

In 1892, the average attendance per day at Port Isaac School was 207. Even when I attended there during the 1950s there were four large classes of children. Our games involved making full use of the characteristics of the playground, and in one particular case, a small cloakroom - 'rough house'!

Big Ones Put Little Ones in Around.

The large playground at Port Isaac School consisted of a larger portion and a smaller one, with a rather narrow area separating them. With this game the older boys put the smaller younger ones in the smaller area. The older boys then formed a line effectively dividing the two areas. The younger boys then had to break through the line to gain access to the larger area. There were no real winners as such. Success was achieved by 'breaking through' the line of boys, and Billy 'Pom Pom' Jnr assures me it was a 'rough and tumble' with the smaller boys having a difficult time breaking through the wall.

Rusty Bum.

This was played in the playground of the old Port Isaac School in the early nineteen thirties and possibly many years before that. It was also played by the girls.

One boy stood with his back against a 'down pipe' on the old Lifeboat House wall. Another boy bent down in front of him, and placed his head on the upright boy's stomach. Another boy then bent forward, and facing the boy already bending down, caught hold of him. Another boy repeated this exercise, and then another until there were as many boys bending down as they wanted. It could be any number. Then a boy started running from the playground wall at the opposite side, and as he approached the line of bcnt over boys he shouted, "Rusty bum here I come, two, four, six, eight, ten ton." The boy then jumped onto the backs of the bent over boys, and got as far forward as possible. The bent over boys then had to hold the boy in position on their backs. Then another boy ran at the line, and shouted the same words before landing on the backs of the boys. This continued until the legs of a boy buckled under the weight of the boys sitting on top of him, and this boy was the loser. Similarly if you fell off you lost. Some boys were very strong, and could hold several on their backs, but no doubt this game would not be allowed in playgrounds today.

Football.

Football was played on Lobber Field, and sometimes matches were played against other teams. Gordon Keat recalls playing in a match at Lostwithiel. Unfortunately in the 1940s 'Boss' Richards the headmaster, fielded a school team which included at least one over-age player who had left the school. As a result of this, the school team was banned from playing competitive matches. During my time at the school between 1951 and 1958, there was no school football team.

Cricket.

George May recalled playing cricket in the narrow section of the playground, however he batted the ball over the cliff so they moved to Lobber to play the game. (Lobber is the large field to the west of Port Isaac Harbour).

Netball.

George also recalled the girls playing netball at school.

Walking on Stilts.

Given the proximity of the playground wall to the cliff, perhaps the most amazing activity allowed at the school was walking on stilts as shown in the photograph.

Children playing on stilts at Port Isaac School playground. No doubt the teachers came up with this novel idea because of the difficulty playing normal games there, but surely this was dangerous near the cliff wall!
From the left: Andrew Bunt, Sarah Gifford, Kim Baker and Mark Dawe.
Courtesy of Redruth Cornish Studies Library.   1975.

Playing Football with Stones in the School Playground.

As people appreciate, the playground is directly above the beach, therefore balls were regularly kicked over the wall and either directly into the sea or on the beach. Sometimes people were strong enough to throw the ball up to the playground from the beach, and Ray Provis was one of those. At other times people walked up the road and handed us the balls through the playground gate, and because of this we very often played football with stones as they stayed near the ground. Surprisingly, this helped to improve our football skills.

Konkaroosha.

This involved folding ones arms, standing on one leg and hopping just in front of your opponent. The object was to knock over your opponent with your folded arms. It was just a bit of fun.

Squashums.

On the side of the school by the bell there was a wall with a corner jutting out. The first person stood in the corner followed by another who tried to force the first person out. Then another child joined the line. Sometimes someone ran at speed at the line, and it became quite painful at times, especially when Barry Cleave decided to take a run at us. I understand that one boy dislocated his shoulder whilst playing this game.

Rough House.

At the rear of the School were the cloakrooms, and the smallest one was a small square room with two doors, one small window and a sink. If anyone was unlucky enough to be nominated for the 'rough house' then the following happened. Someone closed the doors, and another put a garment over the window causing the room to be completely dark. Ten or a dozen boys then stood around the room and pushed the poor victim from side to side until he was quite exhausted. He was then picked up horizontally, head down, and carried to the sink where he was ducked head first in the sink of cold water. He was then carried out into the playground again horizontally, and deposited on the playground tarmac. To say this behaviour would not be allowed today is an understatement. 'Rough House' was still practised whilst I was at the school, and I have to admit I took part in it, although I do not recall being a victim.

Vaulting or Leap frog.

There was nothing unique about this game. Someone bent down and another would leap frog over them. If successful then another person bend down in front of the first, and the child would again attempt to leap frog over the two. The winner was the one who could leap frog the most people.

Rounders.

Once a year, we were allowed to play rounders on Lobber field above the harbour. There was no organized sport at the school whilst I attended it during the 1950s.

A Dangerous Prank.

At Port Isaac School, I recall being picked up and dropped over the playground wall as a prank. There was quite a wide ledge about six feet below the wall on which I landed, but it is not an experience I wish to repeat.

The Girl's and Infant's Playground.

This was much smaller than the boy's area and very enclosed, and the girls asked during fine weather if they could use the larger playground with its fine views of the harbour. Anita Bunt nee Couch recalls in the 1920s playing hopscotch and rounders there, but the girls did not play any of the rough games associated with the boys except for Rusty bum.

Heather Gladstone nee Mitchell, recalls playing rounders there using hands instead of bats during the 1950s. Also she played 'two balls', which involved throwing two balls against an old water tank and juggling them. If a ball was dropped then you were 'out'. Bamboo hoops were placed on the ground, and the girls ran around them and someone would shout 'stop', and it was a rush to see how many could stand inside the hoop.

Against school rules, the girls enjoyed running at a very steep cement slope which is still in place adjacent Fore Street, and climbing to the top where there was a thin ledge. The object was to stay there as long as possible, and then run back down with some difficulty. I recall doing this as an infant, as for a period boys also used this playground.

St Peter's Physical Training Club, Later Port Isaac Youth Club.

At the end of the Second World War, Freddie Ford came to Port Isaac with his wife, and they lived in a bungalow near the council houses in Trewetha Lane, and he started this club which was held in the Church Rooms. Gordon Keat recalls collecting cuttle fish with Terry Thomas which Mr Ford sold to raise funds for the club. Mr Ford purchased a small boat, and went fishing with Tom Strout, but due to a domestic problem, he left Port Isaac rather quickly, and the youth club closed for some time.

Arthur Welch re-started the club which was very popular in the village. Initially it was boys only, but it was open to all regardless of religion. The Anglican Vicar was involved with its organization, and the club boasted a very good boxing ring, parallel bars and box horse. Furthermore a display team made up of club members travelled around local villages giving demonstrations. Mr R Lewin led the badminton; Melville 'Taffy' Watkins the boxing and Mr AE Hillman the administration. However, in October 1953, Mr Welch left the club due to work commitments away, and a letter of thanks was presented to him by the club members. It read as follows: 'The boys of St Peter's Physical Training Club, ask you to accept the accompanying gift as a token of their regard and appreciation of your work among them during the time you have been the instructor of the club'.

The oldest photo I have for St Peter's Youth Club. The boys split the club in half, and played each other on a 'best of three' basis. The first two matches left the teams level, so they named the third and deciding game a cup final. The white team won. The older boys at the club played a similar tournament. This was . when the club was being organized by its founder, Freddie Ford.
Dark players from the left: Roger Worth, Trelights; Gerald.Cheshire, Michael Collings, Len Pluckrose, Warren Dinner, Ernest Tucker, Roger Keat and Joe Knight.
Front row dark players from the left: David Sloggett, Gordon Keat and Mo Tamsett – evacuee.
Light topped players - from the left back row: Les Mitchell, Bert Byfield and Ray Glover.
Middle row from the left: Alan Chadband, Dudley Taylor, Tony Ball, Robert May, Brian Blake, and Brian Richards.
In front: David Short and ?.   *Courtesy of Roger Worth.*   *1946/47.*

As a boy I attended this club which was then organised by Melville 'Taffy' Watkins who lived at 'Treselda', Tintagel Terrace and was a mixed club. 'Taffy' unsurprisingly a Welshman, was sent to Port Isaac to work, and he married Innes Scorey, the daughter of a local coastguard. I have always played sport, and without doubt this was my introduction to table tennis, badminton, boxing and gymnastics.

A good picture showing members of the St Peter's Physical Training Club members visiting Bodmin DCLI. The men in the photo were based at the DCLI School of Languages at Bodmin. The boys seated in the first three rows are from Port Isaac.
Back row of boys from the left: Michael Bate, Roger Keat, James Platt, Tony Robinson, Robert May and Sydney Pluckrose.
Second row of boys from the left: Raymond Bate, Dennis Knight, Brian Nicholls, Anthony Angel, Trevor Platt and Tommy Bradshaw.
Front row of boys: John Welch, David Sherratt, Instructor Arthur Welch of Port Isaac RN, BEM; unknown, Bruce Rowe and Charlie Rowe.
Courtesy of John Welch.   *C 1953.*

St Peter's Physical Training Club Display Team in the middle of a display at an event probably in North Cornwall. It says much for the ability of Arthur Welch to train the local boys to attain a good standard as is evident from this picture. Courtesy of John Welch. C 1953.

Surprisingly all these sports were catered for, and the equipment was generally of very good. In particular the boxing ring was of a very good standard, and that was the only time in my life I donned a pair of boxing gloves and went three rounds against my friends. It did toughen us up however, and helped us survive in what was then quite a tough village. On one occasion the Church Rooms was crowded with local people to see two local young men box; James Platt and Robert May. Both were good boxers, and there was much interest to see who would be the victor. James now lives in Holland, but Robert, a fine young man was later tragically killed on his motor cycle.

The club supplied wood badminton rackets, although when I play today I use modern rackets. 'Taffy' Watkins was an exceptional badminton player, as opponents just could not tell where he intended to place the shuttle.

St Peter's Youth Club's Christmas Show.

At Christmas 1955 the club presented a Christmas Show and entrance was 3d. Part 1. Club swinging exercises were presented by the girls.
Group A: Molly Hook, Mary Rowe, Yvonne Barrow, Nora Keat and Anne Julian.
Group B: Pat Tucker, Pat Lewin, Yvonne Barrow, Susan Osborne and Audrey Collings. The pianist for both was Mrs Porteous.
Other acts included Anne Julian, piano solo; Liza and Georgie, Bucket Song; Nora Keat, West Wind; Club Swingers by the Chief Lead Swinger; Pat and Nora, a piano duet; Jennifer Porteous, Jennifer Martin and Heather Mitchell, an Irish Jig by kind permission of Mrs W Murphy;
Molly, Pat, Audrey, Susan, Nora, Yvonne and Anne, swinging along.

Following the interval a Play was presented entitled 'Captain Souttleboom's Treasure'. The cast was as follows: Captain Souttleboom, Mary Rowe; Black Bill, Nora Keat; Anne Julian, Sharkey Joe; Dennis Knight, the Look-Out-Man; Pat Lewin, Slimy Pete; Trevor Platt, Jamaica Jim; Sidney Pluckrose, Rose Bud; Anne Bartholomew, Mr Fish, (Headmaster of Milchester College). His boys: John Welch, Gordon Hutts, Timothy Osborne and Helen Lewin.
Prompts: Ann Julian and Susan Osborne.
Décor: Adrienne Gunn and Molly Hook.
Stage Assistants: Audrey Collings, Ruth Fairbrother and Molly Hook.
Make-up: Hilda Cowling and Wilma Murphy.
Electrician: Mr Bowden.
Stage Manager: Olive Welch.
Producer: Wilma Murphy.
House Manager: Melvyn Watkins.
Compere: Mr A Hillman.

This is a further example of community activity from a local institution which unfortunately ceased many years ago.

This club was open to all, and there was rarely trouble, the club being an important social meeting place for the local youth, both boys and girls. Few families possessed a television then, and the villagers did their best to make their own entertainment. Today, clubs such as sports and social clubs are struggling to exist, as there is so much modern technology to keep the youth occupied, the result being that unfortunately, that the youth of today are getting insufficient exercise.

Judo Club.

Some local boys started their own judo club in the Church Rooms in the 1960s as the photos demonstrate, but this club did last very long.

Port Isaac Badminton Club.

From about the early 1930s there was a thriving badminton club in the Temperance Hall. Mrs Tom organized a club for girls aged 12 and 13 years in the Temperance Hall during Saturday afternoons, and her husband Leonard assisted.

Members later progressed to the main club, which was organized by Miss Letitia Corkhill. This was a mixed club, and they played matches against other towns such as Launceston and Wadebridge.

When Bessie Selway joined in the early nineteen thirties, the most senior members were Nora Nankivell and Molly Langdon. Emily Kent nee Glover of Dolphin Street regularly won tournaments to the annoyance of some. Many locals were members including Ian Honey, Noreen Honey nee Brown; May Brown, Dick Hocking, Eileen and Mark Prout; John and Mike Scott,

John Welch and Bob Clark pose for a photo outside of the Church Rooms Port Isaac in their judo strip.
Courtesy of John Welch. C 1963.

Harold Brown, Molly Williams, Olive Williams, Joyce Bennett, Dick Brown, Alf and Geoff Taylor, Warren Dinner, D Lewin, Miss Lewin, Nick Bunt, and on occasions, Mark Townsend and Ray Provis. It was held on Monday nights, and it was so popular it was difficult to get a game. Initially they played by oil lamps, and sometimes the shuttles got into the lamps.

Port Isaac Tennis Club.

The club existed during the early 1930s, and they played on one grass court located in a field on Hillson's farm, Trewetha Lane which was owned then by Roy May. The court was situated between the entrance to Hillson Close, and the lane leading to the old farm, or roughly just below where the medical centre is located.

Early members were the Vicar, the Rev Martin; Inys Cory, Murial Couch, Edith Donnithorne, John Tucker, Murial Tucker and Bessie Selway. Roy May played on occasions, and players supplied their own rackets.

I enjoyed a wonderful childhood in the Port Isaac of the fifties and sixties where we enjoyed the wonderful 'outdoors', fantastic beaches, interesting valleys to explore, outdoor games as described in this chapter. Thankfully we were not affected by politically correct theories, and Health and Safety which now affects everyday life in this country. Yes, life is and was a risk, but I am very grateful I had the opportunity of having such a natural childhood at Port Isaac.

The surviving Liberal Club at Port Isaac - please see text.
Photo by Geoff Provis 2013.

Port Isaac Football Team showing off their new kit supplied by M & C Provis, Butchers of Port Isaac. This is just one of the many football teams which have represented Port Isaac over the years, but I do not deal with this subject in this book. Sadly the village has been without a team for several years.
From the left rear: Brian Richards, Nigel Sherratt, Bob Franklin, Steve Bunt, Kevin Richards and Peter Rowe.
Middle row from the left: Les Honey, Tony Provis, John Brown, Jimmy Langton, Mark Thomas, Trevor Haynes, and Quentin Black.
Front row from the left: Kevin Grills, Richard Fisher, Mark Provis who supplied the kit; Kim Flitney and Trevor Grills.
Courtesy of Peter Rowe.   C 1990.

Port Isaac Liberal Club.

Building commenced in 1911, although the local fish merchants offered a cellar in Roscarrock Hill for this purpose. Delabole Liberal Club assisted with furnishings, and an open fire place was provided. Games played at the club included snooker, cards, bagatelle, whist and draughts, and a spittoon was provided for the men. Dick Rowe and Fletcher Sweet often played each other at draughts, and rows and arguments were commonplace, especially about politics. Dick was very good at draughts, and once beat the champion of Liverpool. Syd Remick was the caretaker of the club at the start of the Second World War. His family suffered greatly during the two World Wars, and it seems so unfair that a thoroughly decent Port Isaac family suffered such tragedy. Captain Callaway was also a caretaker.

Remarkably, this club is still functioning in much the same manner as before. Over the years various locals have helped organize the club, and during the early years of the twentieth century if someone in the village died, the flag which flew outside the club flew at half-mast.

No alcohol was consumed on the premises, and the main feature of the club is a snooker table which originated from the old Conservative Club at Port Isaac. This club could fairly be described as an almost lone survivor from the olden days, but as with many such institutions, it is in need of new members.

Port Isaac Minors played in a North Cornwall Minor League, and we were the youngest team in it, thereby losing the majority of our games.
Back row from the left: Ken Couch, the son of a local coastguard; David Sherratt, Jeremy Hicks, (Boscastle); Robin Rivers, (Camelford); Jim Hocking and Timothy Osborne.
Front row from the left: Geoff Provis, Eric Donnithorne, Alan Short, Colin Chegwyn, (Camelford) and Barry Collins. I remember well playing against Wadebridge and St Kew Minors. Colin Chegwyn became one of the finest players Cornwall has produced, playing numerous times for Cornwall, Truro, Falmouth and other senior teams. Our home pitch was the same as the senior team, the field now containing the new Port Isaac car park.
Courtesy of Sarah Cook nee Hicks and Colin Chegwyn. About 1956/57.

Port Isaac Lost Societies.

Over many years, much concern has been expressed at Port Isaac about history being lost, and this is one of the concerns which led to me writing this series of books. As if to prove this point, I have found reference to a number of old societies that certainly existed at Port Isaac, but the headquarters of these various societies could find no official record of them. Furthermore, senior locals appear to have no knowledge of a few of them. Terry Knight of the St Agnes Old Cornwall Society feels that one reason may be the outbreak of the Second World War, when much paper work was pulped for the war effort. Another reason may be the historical lack of a society at Port Isaac for recording local history, such as a museum.

Similarly, some sporting events appear to have been lost in the 'mists of time'. The following are a few of these societies and events:

Port Isaac Royal British Legion.

There is no record of a Port Isaac Royal British Legion at the legion headquarters. However, in the Western Morning News of the 8th August 1925 the following report appeared:

'The Port Isaac branch of the Royal British Legion organised a carnival and concert in aid of the Lifeboat Institution on Wednesday. A procession headed by the Camelford band marched down to Port Gaverne, and back to Port Isaac to the assembling ground where the prizes were distributed.

A concert which was held in the Church Rooms in the evening proved popular, and the hall was packed. Following the concert there was a dance'.

A little later in this book you will read that in May 1935, Mr SJ Honey of Port Isaac was the hon. secretary of the Port Isaac British Legion, so why is there no reference to this branch at their headquarters? It appears from the above that it existed for at least ten years, but is it significant that it was the period leading up to World War Two? I have not been able to ascertain where they met.

Port Isaac Old Cornwall Society.

By pure chance whilst researching Port Isaac, I came across a mention of a Port Isaac Old Cornwall Society. I was unaware this existed, and Terry Knight of St Agnes informed me that it was not listed with the head office of that society. However, two old magazines there did mention that Mr WL Whiffin of Khandalla, Port Isaac as being the secretary, and another magazine in 1933 referred to the first talk to be given to the society that year by Edmund H Hambly. The official colour of the society was red, and I have made the cover of this book red in memory of this lost society.

The following report appeared in the Devon and Cornwall Post of the 16th April 1932: 'The first meeting of the Port Isaac Old Cornwall Society was held in the Church Rooms last week, and there was a good attendance. The Vicar was in the chair'.

The first meeting of the Port Isaac Old Cornwall
Society was held in St Peter's Church Rooms during the first week of April 1932. However, its existence was
unfortunately very brief, probably because of the outbreak of the Second World War. If it had continued, perhaps much more of Port Isaac's history would now be preserved.
Photo by Geoff Provis.   2012.

The Western Morning News of the 7th June 1932 gives a report concerning a visit by the St Austell Old Cornwall Society to St Endellion and Port Isaac. The following is an excerpt relating to Port Isaac:

'At Port Isaac the society was met by Mrs Hambly, and Mr HW Whiffin of the newly formed Old Cornwall Society, and later by the Rev WT Martyn, the President. Mr Martyn had been the Vicar of Port Isaac from the time it constituted a separate parish from St Endellion. Members of the visiting society saw many of the interesting old world charms of this fishing haven, the entrance to the smugglers cave under the kitchen of the Golden Lion Inn, Temple Bar, the Market, together with most delightful peeps of quaint old houses and back ways. St Ives and Polperro were likened, but, with Port Isaac, each has its particular points of interest'.

This is a further example of another society which existed at Port Isaac, of which there is no official record at that society's headquarters. Perhaps if this society had survived, then much more local history would have been recorded and preserved, as this is the main objective of such societies. Hopefully my books may help to recover some lost ground.

Note also that Temple Bar was referred to using its correct name, not the name 'Squeeze Belly Alley', which was attributed to it in the 1950s.

Port Isaac United Church Clubland.

During the Second World War, when there were many evacuees living locally, a number of Port Isaac institutions joined together to form the United Church Clubland. These included the Boy's Brigade, Methodist Youth Club and Boy's First Aid Class. The president was the Rev Martyn, and the secretary Miss Smyth a school teacher. Frances Larkin a lady with experience of being a county youth organizer assisted. (TS).

St Endellion Scout Association.

The scout associations were aligned with churches, and St Endellion Church formed the Port Isaac scouts using the name of the St Endellion Scout Association. The headquarters of that association has supplied me with the following details:

Mr C Parmee of Port Isaac - Scout Master 19th March 1913.

Mr Sercombe of Port Isaac - instructor, 27th March 1913.

Doctor WR Jackson of Port Isaac - instructor, 25th September 1913.

Mr MA Robinson of Ashworth House Port Isaac - instructor on 25th September 1913, and Assistant Scout Master on 16th October 1913.

Miss MA Hyde of Port Isaac - Scout Master on 1st January 1914.

Mr C Parmee of Port Isaac as Hon Scout Master on 1st January 1914.

The society ceased sometime between 1921 and 1922, and no scout troops were registered after the First World War.

Port Isaac Army Cadets.

Just after the Second World War, the 'big thing' for the older boys was the newly formed army cadets, but it did not last very long, as everyone was fed up with uniforms and war games. Vic 'Boss' Richards, the school master; Colonel Genders who lived in Trewetha Lane; and Cyril Kinnings the cobbler were the cadet leaders.

There were about fifteen members, and they marched and drilled in the area known as 'Little Hill', Fore Street, Port Isaac. My eldest cousin Tony Gill was a corporal, and meetings were held in the Methodist Sunday School at Roscarrock Hill. The boys also practiced boxing.

Port Isaac Working Mens' Institute.

In the Western Morning News of the 24th April 1935, there is a brief report relating to a Working Mens' Institute at Port Isaac. The following is a quote from this report: 'In the small Working Mens' Institute at Port Isaac this afternoon, Mr EW Gill, the County Coroner for Bodmin and District, will conduct an inquest etc'.

I have checked with the headquarters of the Working Mens' Institutes, but they have no record of a branch at Port Isaac. I have also asked some older residents if they have

The old Port Isaac Working Men's Institute met above the Old Bark House, Dolphin Street in a room which later became the Dole Office. This property is now used for purposes other than family habitation, along with every other property in Dolphin Street except one.
Photo taken by Geoff Provis.   2013.

any knowledge of this society, but to no avail. However, the late Joe Rowe stated that the large room above the Bark House in Dolphin Street was the location for the Working Men's Club. This later became a dole office, a branch of the Camelford office.

Port Isaac 'Blue Waves' Football Club for Boys.

This club was started sometime around 1930 by Leonard Tom who then resided in the village, but I have no further details of it. It certainly possessed an interesting name.

Port Isaac Branch of the British and Foreign Bible Society.

The Royal Cornwall Gazette of 1848 states, 'four hundred and thirty eight Bibles and Testaments distributed by associations at Wadebridge, St Minver, Port Isaac and Camelford during the preceding year'.

This is very interesting, and shows that there was a demand for Christianity at Port Isaac which at that time was experiencing extreme hardship. This society was formed in 1804 initially to provide Bibles to Welsh speaking Christians, because there was a lack of affordable Bibles.

Bessie Selway informed me that the Port Isaac Bible Society met once annually at the Temperance Hall, but I have no further details of their activities, but I presume their main task was the distribution of Bibles. The formation of the Port Isaac Choral Society was first mooted at these meetings.

Port Isaac Rechabites.

The Rechabites were a friendly society, and the Port Isaac branch met in the Odd Fellows Hall at the Wesleyan Chapel during the 1930s and 1940s. This hall was situated below the Sunday School. Paul Welsh, who was originally from Wadebridge was in charge , and he resided in the new council houses in Trewetha Lane. The monthly fee to be a member was five pence ha'penny, and the main object was to allow families to pay for a doctor or a dentist should the need arise, or to pay out a certain amount should the member be sick.

In the meeting there was a long table, and members wore a ribbon which came down to a point around their necks. The ribbon stated whatever office the person held. After the meeting there was a social evening for the children organized by Mr Welsh, and games were played. Mr Welsh was very kind and popular with the children. It was also a Temperance Society, and they were not supposed to drink alcohol.

Every twelve months exams were taken, and most children gained 2nd or 3rd certificates, but Mr Welsh's daughters always received a 1st.

Temperance Blue Ribbonists of Port Isaac. Royal Cornwall Gazette 30th May 1884.

'Blue Ribbonists of Port Isaac held a festival on Friday. Headed by the Delabole Brass Band, the members and friends paraded the place during the afternoon, and at five o'clock, a public tea was held in the United Methodist Free Church school room.

Later there was a public meeting which was well attended. Short and appropriate addresses were delivered by the Rev J Cleave and H Fry, (Free Church). The meeting was enlivened by the able rendering of various pieces from Sankey and Moody's collection by a mixed choir'.

For further details on the Blue Ribbon movement, see the section on chapels at Port Isaac.

Port Isaac Conservative Club.

There is no official record of this club, but it is common knowledge with local people that it did exist. A secretary of the Association of Conservative Clubs informed me that the club did not have a reference number, therefore it is possible they did not register their membership. The snooker table of the club was taken to the new Liberal Club at Port Isaac in 1911, so I presume that was possibly its date of closure. No alcohol was served there, but games such as cards, draughts and snooker were played in a similar manner to the surviving Liberal Club. The building was converted into a bungalow, and was then owned by Ewart Worden. Ewart's sister lived there with her husband Harold Kent, previously of Trelights, who was a butcher. Joe Saundry later converted it into a very nice house, and he said there was only one window in the whole of the back of the building, making it rather dark.

Port Isaac Conservative Club. This house is the last building in the built up area,
on the right going up Church Hill. It was built on the old club house which was a
slightly smaller building.
Photo taken by Geoff Provis.   2013.

Port Isaac Conservative Reading Room.

The ground floor of Rowe's Paper Shop in Fore Street, was once the Port Isaac Conservative Reading Room up until about 1917. Many of the older generation men met there, and games were played such as draughts and darts. Occasionally the men sat around a fire arguing about politics, and their voices gradually increased in volume until Mrs Rowe picked up a broom, turned it upside-down and gave the floor some heavy bangs with it. Then the arguing subsided.

Port Isaac's Original Sports Centre.

Many years ago, a room in a cottage in Middle Street, Port Isaac was used by the locals for wrestling and other games, and Joe Saundry's father, Tom, wrestled there. This cottage is the last cottage on the left before entering the ruins of the old Wesleyan Chapel at the end of Middle Street. The room used was on the ground floor, and nearest the chapel. I do not know how this cottage became to be so used.   In the very early years of the twentieth century, the cottages at Port Isaac were in such a dreadful state that the village was condemned, with plans made to demolish everything in the old part of the village. At that time it was possible to purchase property for as little as £5 or £10, and during this period, some cottages were abandoned, and some families claimed properties and also land as their own, although I shall not mention names. It may be in the case above, that the locals simply made use of an empty cottage for their own sporting purposes.

This cottage was then situated in the portion of Middle Street previously named Chapel Street.

Port Isaac Bible Christian Society.

Between 1818 and 1839, a Bible Christian Society existed at Port Isaac, but they were never able to build or purchase a building for a chapel, hence their relatively brief existence.   They met in a room of a cottage and its location is unknown. (TS).

Port Isaac Toc H Branch.

Strictly speaking this is not really a 'lost society', as it was functioning within living memory, and indeed was active when I was a child. However, I include it in this section as there is no record of it at Toc H Headquarters, and history of it appears to be very sparse.

On the 26th July 1952, the Port Isaac Toc H Branch organised the Port Isaac Carnival, and then the President was Mr CP Symons Esq; the Chairman H Spry, no doubt Harold; the Hon Treasurer W Dyer, probably Bill Dyer the village Policeman; and Mr A E Hillman, the proprietor of Chapman's of Fore Street, Port Isaac. The competitors assembled in Mr Blake's field and there were seventeen entry classes.

That evening, 'carnival night', three 'grand dances' all commencing at 8 30pm were held as follows: The Duchy Dance Band with their electric claviolili, played at the Temperance Hall, the MC being Mr AE Hillman; the Rivolians performed at the Rivoli Dance Hall, Mr Brimacombe being the MC; the Robertsons played at an 'Old Tyme Dance' at the Church Rooms, the MC being Mr H Goss, and during the afternoon Wadebridge Town Band played on the beach. In addition, at 2.30pm there was a Coastguard display and water sports on Port Isaac Beach, and a balloon race from the Town Platt.

Briefly; the Toc H movement, 'seeked to ease the burden of others through acts of charity'. They also organized local charitable activities such as the above carnival.

Port Isaac Conservative Reading Room in Fore Street, Port Isaac. This became Rowe's Paper Shop, and is now a shop named Fearless.
Photo taken by Geoff Provis.   2013.

This small cottage near the old Wesleyan Chapel in Middle Street, previously Chapel Street, was taken over by the locals for use as a small sports centre, and activities such as wrestling occurred there.
Picture taken by Geoff Provis.   2010.

The Smiling Sardine restaurant was previously known as the Toc H Rooms. In the 1950s it was also used by the St John's Ambulance Brigade.
Photo taken by Geoff Provis.   2013.

Port Isaac Quakers or Society of Friends.

The Quakers were formed in 1654, and are also known as a Religious Society of Friends. They are of a Protestant tradition, and were founded by George Fox. Their beliefs include pacifism, refusal to fight in wars, refusal to own slaves and prison reform. In England they were persecuted for refusing to attend Church of England services and to pay tithes, and they have a long history at Port Isaac. Quakers were active at Port Isaac during John Wesley's visits in the mid eighteenth century.

Brook Cottage in Middle Street, Port Isaac. This property I have been informed, was used by Port Isaac Quakers for their meetings, but I have been unable to find proof of this. Photo taken from near the pump. Note the Carriage House on the right.
Photo taken by Geoff Provis. 2013.

The Cornwall Record Office contains records of Port Isaac Quaker meetings, but some are difficult to read and they give no clue as to the location of their meeting house. I have been told by an elderly resident that Brook Cottage in Middle Street was so used, but I have no proof of this.

Port Isaac Annual Regatta.

In the days of sail, Port Isaac held its own annual regatta, when boats from Newquay and Padstow visited to take part in the races. Working sailing luggers and pilot gigs raced against each other, no doubt helping the locals to form friendships between the visiting communities. The numbers of spectators travelling by horse drawn transport from Newquay and Padstow can only be guessed at. No doubt some travelled by sea in the competing vessels.

On the 27th May 1871, the following report appeared in the Royal Cornwall Gazette.

'The Port Isaac Annual Regatta was held on Friday, but the boat contest - one of the principal features at previous regattas - was wanting on this occasion, owing to the large number of crafts hauled up for painting, and in consequence of which, one of the boats and a pretty little yacht from Padstow were the only competitors in the solitary sailing match that took place.

The yacht was the *Southerner* (Hon A Arundel), and the boat *Harriett,* (Capt W Hosking). The former came in first, but the owner handed over the prize to the other competitor. The next contest was between 5 six-oared gigs over a distance of four and a half miles. This was a well contested race, and great interest was felt in it as much rivalry has for several years existed between the gigs of the various places.

The boats came in as follows:-

Constance, (Knight), Padstow. 1st £2.10s, 37 mins 45 secs.

Tom Sayers, (May), Port Isaac, 2nd £1.10s, 38 mins 53 secs.
Treffry, (Carne), Newquay, 3rd 15s, 38 mins 55 secs.
Excelsior, (Brokenshire), Padstow, 10s, 41 mins.
Rescue, (Stribley), Padstow 42 mins 50 secs'.

I have spent numerous hours talking to older Port Isaac persons over the years about maritime matters, and I have not heard any mention of an annual Port Isaac regatta. Perhaps interest in the event waned, as you will note above that the boats were hauled upon the Town Platt for painting. I am sure that if the locals were keen to take part in the regatta, then the boats would have been ready to partake.

Port Isaac Branch of the Royal Camelford and Bottreaux Odd Fellows Lodge.

It is common knowledge among Port Isaac people, that the large room beneath the Wesleyan Sunday School was named 'Odd Fellows Hall'. However I was not aware of the exact nature of the Port Isaac Odd Fellows. A report in the Royal Cornwall Gazette of 22nd July 1876 states that the Port Isaac Odd Fellows were a branch of the above lodge. This report gives interesting details of a fete and a gig race as follows:

'The Port Isaac Branch of the Royal Camelford and Bottreaux Odd Fellows Lodge held a fete at Port Isaac on Wednesday week which proved in every way a success. The bretheran after perambulating the town accompanied by a brass band, sat down to a capitol tea provided in Odd Fellows Hall. In connection with the fete, a regatta took place for 'six oared' gigs.

Since the regatta held in May, and at Padstow on Whit Tuesday, a great deal of chaff and challenge between the Padstow and Port Isaac crews has taken place which brought three boats from Padstow on Wednesday to compete against the Port Isaac boat *Tom Sayers*. After a most exciting race, (7 miles), *Tom Sayers,* (Phillips) came in 1st, won by 30 seconds; 2nd *Teaser* (Rawle); 3rd *Hero,* (Cowl); and 4th *May Flower,* (Stribley)'.

A most interesting account; and it also refers to a Port Isaac Regatta held in May of that year. Clearly, with a brass band, a set tea and a gig race, our ancestors believed in enjoying themselves on such occasions.

In 1872, the following Port Isaac men were officers of the Camelford and Bottreaux Lodge, and clearly represented the interests of Port Isaac: Brother Mark Guy, and Brother Trevan; Surgeon for the Port Isaac district. (Devon & Cornwall Post 6th December 2012).

For information, the Independent Order of Odd Fellows began in 18th century England. It was deemed 'odd' to find people organized for the purpose of giving aid to those in need without recognition, and pursuing projects for the benefit of mankind.

So this is another society operating in 'old' Port Isaac to assist those in need. This is a far cry indeed from the situation in 2013, where the vast majority of properties in 'old' Port Isaac are used as 'holiday homes', 'letting properties', or simply an item on the property portfolio of 'well heeled' investors from afar. Whilst I do not wish to return to the days of poverty, surely to allow a whole culture to disappear is a retrograde step. I feel some official action was necessary to protect such communities as Port Isaac, as unfortunately the local Port Isaac Cornish community has become a 'lost society'. The presence of a few local Cornish people does not alter this fact.

The subject of 'lost society' is a feature of all my books, and none is more striking than the present state of the 'old' village of Port Isaac. Even in my youth in the 1950s and 60s, the older men met and talked or 'yarned' about village events. This helped give the village its unique character. Now, these scenes simply do not exist. Similarly, in every cottage and in every street there were mainly local people who knew each other and who conversed with each other. That close community may accurately be described as a 'lost society'. Recently, a Port Isaac lady now in her seventies visited the old part of the village for the first time in ten years, and then asked to be taken to her present home as she was in tears. She said to me later, "What have they done to our village. I used to be proud to say I was from Port Isaac, now look at it."
These local men are 'yarning' at Little Hill, Fore Street, Port Isaac.
From the left: John Bray Honey, Ned Cowling, possibly Warwick Bishop, Edward Williams, John Provis, the great-grandfather of the author and harbourmaster; Mr Smith, Lawrence Smith's father; Andy Oaten and unknown.
Courtesy of Merle Arnold nee Honey.   Early 1930s. (The wall behind was built in the early 1930s).

More Local Characters.

I must again explain that when using direct speech in the following text, I spell words incorrectly, and use poor grammar occasionally, in order that the speech may sound authentic.

Warwick Provis and Jack Thomas.

During the early 1930s, Jim Sweet was tending to his boat the *Irene,* which was on its moorings and 'aground' in Port Isaac Harbour. Jim climbed inside the boat to unscrew the plug to let out the water which had accumulated overnight. After he climbed inside, a group of boys including Warwick Provis and Jack Thomas, who were having a break from school, pulled the cover back over the boat, and tied it firmly to the gunwhale, thereby leaving poor Jim trapped inside. The Headmaster Vic Richards later administered the cane to the boys.

Jackie 'Diamonds' Hosking.

During the 1930s, Jackie 'Diamonds' Hosking of Roscarrock Hill, Port Isaac, helped with the organisation of the Liberal Club. One day, Henry Scorey, a teenager and his mates were in the club using some bad language.

Jackie 'Diamonds' shouted at them, "If you b-----s dun't stop swearin, I'll kick the b----y lot of ee out."

Leonard Collings, Sam Bate and the Chamber Pot.

I shall tell this as it was told to me by Joe Saundry:

'Years ago Port Isaac men went yachtin in the summer months, and they got the train to Portsmouth, but t'was too late to get on their yacht so they got digs. Well Leonard and Sam got their digs. They went to the pub in the evenin, ad several to drink and returned to their digs late.

Sam got up in the night and said to Leonard, "This ere pot's gettin full up."

Leonard said, "Well yank un out the winda."

Sam picked the pot up, gave un a good yank, but the andle come off and the pot rolled down a galvanised roof. Under the galvanised roof there wuz an oss tied up, and the oss kicked the side of the shed in. I dun't knaw what happened next, but they joined the yacht next day'.

Norman 'Ningy' Short and the Boxing Match.

Norman was well known for contorting his face into many different angles and expressions, hence his other nickname, 'Gurnin'.

As a young man Norman boxed and wrestled occasionally, including at boxing exhibitions held at Wadebridge Town Hall, and locals were allowed to box as challengers for a fee of 30/-. One night a challenger did not appear, so the Port Isaac men asked Norman to have a go. He did so, and during the fight he told his Port Isaac mates that he was having a hiding. He then made up a face whilst sitting in his corner, and kept the face contorted whilst waiting for the next round. His opponent

Ann Smith a regular visitor to Port Isaac poses for a photo with Norman 'Ningy' Short on the left, and Tom Saundry on the right. The Smiths were good friends with the two local men and John Glover. In fact many locals made good friends with such visitors. I have however, heard complaints from the regular loyal visitors, that Port Isaac is just not the same as the village they grew to love, and they despair at the loss of the local characters.
Courtesy of Ann Smith.   *C 1964.*

Frank 'Rosie' Roseveare pictured with his wife. 'Rosie' accurately forecast the fate of Port Isaac many years ago.
Courtesy of Reuben Roseveare.   *C 1930.*

thought he had him defeated such was the sight of 'Ningy's' tortured or injured face, but 'Ningy' came out for the second round, hit his opponent hard and won the fight.

Norman usually carried a pocket full of 'one penny' chewing gums, plus 6" lengths of twist tobacco which he tied into a knot, prior to putting it into his mouth.

Frank 'Rosie' Roseveare – True Prediction.

About 65 years ago, 'Rosie' said to his Grandson Reuben Roseveare when referring to Port Isaac, "You watch it boy, later on they'll want to turn this place into a playground fer they up there."

Mary and William of Port Quin.

The following is a story related by my Grandfather Anthony Provis:

'Many years ago a married couple living at Port Quin did not have a happy married life. Mary said it was William's fault, and William said it was Mary's, so a Minister paid them a visit to see if he could make the peace between them. At the time of calling William was out, so he had a talk with Mary. He then found William,

Jackie 'Diamonds' Hosking yarning on the Town Platt with Captain Sammy Keat. Jackie for a period helped out at the Port Isaac Liberal Club.
Courtesy of Gordon Keat.   C 1945.

Joe Saundry spent his life at Port Isaac working as a general builder. He was a very thorough methodical tradesman, with a good sense of humour, and he helped me with information for this book.
Photo taken by Geoff Provis.   C 2004.

and to weigh things up he thought Mary was most to blame, so using a Biblical term he said to Mary, "You must heap coals of fire on William's head."

She said, "I embm tried that, but I've poured boilin water on un.'"

Dick Rowe's Advice on Divorce and Marriage.

On divorce: 'If one id'n enough, twenty id'n too many'.

On marriage: 'Never get married till you've weathered un, summer an winter'.

Port Isaac Locals.

During World War Two, a small wreck occurred near Port Isaac. After the locals had helped themselves to flour and chocolate, they informed the Coastguard Mr Rook of the wreck site, and he said to them, "You b.....s."

'Dreckly'.

My Uncle Ray Provis took a 'party' of visitors out mackerel fishing, which involved towing a 'hand line' behind the boat.

A visitor said to Ray, "When do we pull the line in?"

Ray said, "Dreckly."

The silly visitor pulled the line in straight away!!!

Jack Collings Cleaning Ann Steer's Grave Stone.

Ann Steer was a midwife at Port Isaac during the early twentieth century. Many years later, Bill Steer visited St Endellion Churchyard, and he noticed Jack Collings cleaning Ann's gravestone. Bill knew he was not being paid to do so, so he politely asked Jack why he was doing it.

Jack replied, "Ann brought all the Collings family into the world for nothin, and we couldn't afford to pay her."

This was an example of the community spirit at Port Isaac many years ago, and an incident which says much for the character of Jack Collings, and indeed Ann Steer.

'Gaggy' and 'Teddybush'.

'Gaggy' Hosking was the step son of Edward 'Teddybush' Hosking, and they both lived at Roscarrock Hill, Port Isaac. 'Gaggy' often collected stones off of Port Isaac Beach so that he and 'Teddybush' could throw them at each other when they had a row.

Captain Tom May made the Sparks Fly.

After the sailing ship trade finished, Captain Tom May Jnr farmed at Bodannon Farm, and he was in the habit of spending some time at the Golden Lion pub. When he did so he tied his horse to the telegraph pole outside the pub door in Fore Street, and this pole is still there. When he came out of the pub, he jumped on his horse, dug his heels in and the horse galloped up Fore Street making sparks fly off the road stone.

'Teddybush' Wanted to Fight Everyone.

Edward 'Teddybush' Hosking was on a yacht with Dick Rowe. One night 'Teddy' got back drunk and wanted to fight everyone on the yacht including Dick. Dick didn't say anything, but he picked 'Teddy' up, and threw him over his shoulders straight into his bunk.

The next morning 'Teddy' said to Dick, "You broke me back Dick Raw."

Dick said, "If you cause any more trouble I'll break yer neck as well."

There was no more trouble after that.

Mrs Wearne nee Cowling of Pendoggett Became Flustered.

Soon after World War Two, John Charles Hawken, a local farmer, visited the Post Office at Pendoggett for some petrol. The pumps there were of the 'wind up' variety operated by Mrs Wearne nee Cowling, who had only recently married for the first time at about the age of fifty.

Edith Wearne nee Cowling, standing outside her Post office at Pendoggett. She became very flustered when John Charles Hawken asked her what it was like to be married! Courtesy of Win Leverton nee Cleave.   Before 1950.

He ordered an amount, and when the dial reached the mark he said to her, "What's it like bein married then? What's it like avin a man about the house?"

She got so flustered she forgot to charge him for the fuel or ask for his ration coupons.

Port Gaverne's Bulldog.

In the early 1950s, Dick and Bessie Atkinson resided at the 'art – deco'house, Port Gaverne. Much to the amusement and fascination of local youths, their bulldog regularly walked around with a pet monkey on its back.

Hannah Jones of Lower Trefreock.

Hannah was originally from 'Spring Cottage' Trelights, and I recall as a young boy occasionally seeing her. She was an old short lady who gave the appearance of being very poor, and she regularly trudged up Church Hill to her cottage at Lower Trefreock. She had a hard life, and many people in Port Isaac gave her free meals. She did washing for various people including Bessie Steer, Mark Bishop's daughter. Because of her deafness, Hannah often talked to herself and sometimes she also answered for the people she was talking to. When she met Bessie Steer, the conversation was sometimes as follows with Hannah saying, "How's Mrs Steer, Mrs Steer's alright, yea, Mrs Steer's alright."

Hannah was very good natured, and probably as a result of her deafness, expert at lip reading, and she could see well in the dark. On one occasion, she stood in Rowe's paper shop talking to Mrs Rowe, and looking out of the window at a lady talking in a shop across the road. After this lady stopped talking, Hannah proceeded to tell Mrs Rowe all the gossip she had learned by 'lip reading' this lady.

Edwin Bunt of Trelights.

As a youngster Edwin walked through Port Isaac wearing a bowler hat. A local boy took off Edwin's hat and stamped on it.

Edwin said, "I hit'n so ard boy, t'was like an oss kickin."

Dennis Knight saved a Life and was Paid 2/6d.

Looking after fishermen's punts in Port Isaac Harbour was popular with young boys, and I spent many hours doing so. This simply involved sculling or rowing the punts around the harbour usually while the fisherman was at sea. One day, Dennis saved Lloyd

Edwin Bunt on the left and his father John Bunt, blacksmiths of Trelights pictured near their smithy. Edwin was not amused when a Port Isaac boy stamped on his bowler hat when he was a youth.
Courtesy of Roger Worth, Edwin's grandson.   C 1925.

Polkinghorne's life whilst doing so, so I shall let Dennis continue:

'Lloyd was a bit younger than me, and he had Tommy Tabb's punt and I had Sammy Dyer Thomas's. Lloyd sculled right across my bow and my punt went straight into his. He went over and down; then he come up and went down again. The next time he came up, I grabbed him and dragged him out, took him on the beach and doubled him over. He started gasping and spewing up water, and then he went off. Now you must understand, 2/6 was a lot of money back then, but only twelve and half pence now. A bit later, Nona, Lloyd's mother gave me 2/6 for saving Lloyd's life'.

Jimmy Vickery – It'll cost ee an ounce of Baccy.

I mentioned in my book 'The Fishermen of Port Isaac', how Jimmy Vickery sat in the doorway of his cottage in Appletree Court, Church Hill. Visitors stopped and stared at this old man looking out his doorway, and some asked him if they could photograph him. Jimmy always said, "You can take a phota, but t'will cost ee an ounce of baccy."

Jim Honey and John Mills – Two Very Strong Local Fishermen.

A visitor parked his car next to the Town Platt against the advice of local fishermen who told him he was partially obstructing the slipway. The visitor ignored their advice, so John Mills and Jim Honey lifted his car onto the Platt, depositing it between small boats so that it could not be moved.

Anthony Provis Went to Chapel but got a Shock.

Maurice Brown, a Methodist stalwart, was telling a ghost story at the Sunday school one evening which involved him gradually lowering his voice as the lights were being dimmed. Anthony Provis, my grandfather, noticed the lights going dim from outside, so he went into the chapel, which was next door to the Sunday school to investigate. He walked slowly towards the Sunday school and opened a door between the two rooms. Meanwhile, Maurice was reaching the pinnacle of his story which involved him grabbing the door handle and screaming. However he did not realise Anthony was standing in the doorway in the darkness, so instead of the handle he grabbed my grandfather's ...... (Censored).

Anthony 'Antny' Provis, the harbour master on the left, leaning on the winch which was used to haul fishing boats onto the Platt and having a 'yarn' with Bill Cowling. The small box on top of the winch was used to place the car parking fees for cars using the Platt. At that time, cars did not park on the beach. 'Granfer' suffered quite a shock when he went to check the chapel!
Courtesy of Carol Brogan-Taylor nee Provis.   C 1955.

Tommy Sherratt the Organ Blower.

In the 1930s, young Tommy Sherratt was blowing the organ at the Methodist Chapel Port Isaac, when he secretly asked David Hoskin to stand in for him. However, he forgot to tell David that when the pressure mark reached the top he must stop blowing. Therefore when the mark reached the top David kept blowing, and the organ pipes started to screech.

David said, "Grannie Tucker the organist was not amused."

Captain 'Billy' Mitchell of Port Isaac.

Captain Mitchell was the master of the schooner *Bessy Jane* during the second half of the nineteenth century, and he was very short but immensely strong, being able to lift two 56 lb weights sideways to above his head during his younger days. One day whilst in port at Dublin, a local tried to sell Billy his own anchor, so he promptly threw the errant Irishman overboard.

Andy Oaten and His 'Yarns'.

Andy was fond of telling little yarns and 'catching people out'. The following are two examples:

He would pick on someone and say, "The moon's made of green cheese or tid'n, but tid'n is it?"

The person replied, "No."

Andy said, "So tis then ind'n it?"

Andy's favourite story was as follows:

'Three men go to a restaurant, ave a meal for £10 each, and they give £30 to a waiter. The waiter goes to his boss who said he should give um £5 back. The waiter realises they embn given him a tip, so he gives um £1 each, and keeps £2 for his-self.

So the waiter gives um £1 each, which means they've paid £9 each for the meal. 3 x £9 = £27. Add the £2 the waiter keeps = £29'.

Work it out yourself.

Andy also regularly walked at high water mark on Port Isaac beach if there was 'ground sea' pounding the shore, and regularly claiming he could find gold dubloons. To support his claims, a report in the Western Morning News of 1st February 1929 states, 'Andy Oaten finds gold coin the size of a sixpence. On one side is the inscription, "Glory God in the highest"'.

John Hicks and His Bullock.

One day Joan Dustow and her sister were walking over Church Hill, and John Hicks with a bullock was walking towards them. Suddenly the bullock started running towards them, and then without warning it stopped. The girls asked John how it stopped in such a fashion, and John said, "I prayed and you were saved."

Gladys and Jane Mitchell.

My Gran Gladys Provis nee Mitchell, often attended chapel as a teenager with her sister Jane, but they did not like the sermons. One Sunday they decided to sit straight in front of and below the pulpit, so that the preacher could not see them. However, much to their annoyance, the preacher had a turn in an eye, and during the sermon this eye was staring down at both of them, giving them uncontrollable fits of the giggles.

Minesweeper's Searchlight Searched for Tony Gill and Ian Honey.

Just after the Second World War, Tony Gill and Ian 'Bunny' Honey, decided to scull a punt out to a minesweeper which was just off of Port Isaac. As they sculled back, the lights of Port Isaac were extinguished as there were still shortages, and the boys could not see their way back. Fortunately, the minesweeper sailors recognized their predicament, and switched on their searchlight and searched the coastline until they spotted the punt. They then guided it into Port Isaac.

Fishermen Poets, as Told by Frank Rowe Snr to Joe Saundry.

In previous days, Appletree Cottages off Church Hill were occupied by all local people, mainly fishermen. One or two of the cottages were built on top the other, and Jimmy Creighton's and Sammy 'Dyer' Thomas's cottages were so built. It was in the days of sail, and in the mornings both would look out their windows to see if it was 'dirty weather', and if it was fit to go 'out sea'.

If it was unfit, Jimmy shouted to Sammy, "Light the fire Sammy 'Dyer'."

Sammy then shouted back, "Fry the bacon Jimmy Creighton."

Now this may seem a rather simple affair to the casual reader of this book, but good humour was abundant in old Port Isaac even though times were tough. Furthermore, it mattered not that they were prepared to repeat this simple poem on other days if the weather was rough. Most of us are 'creatures of habit', but in an isolated insular village such as Port Isaac, people became known by their customs and habits much more so than in 2013.

The men continually kept an eye on the weather, as their lives and livelihood depended on it, and men such as Frank Rowe Snr were expert weather forecasters, and a local farmer, Horace Hillson, a farmer, also excelled at this. Weather satellites had not been invented in those days.

Will Avery Regularly Exaggerated his Gardening Skills.

Will was a Port Gaverne fisherman, and very strong, but he was well known for exaggerating the size and quality of his gardening produce.

He once said to some friends, "Grew a cabbage once, t'was that big, took four men to lift un into Taylor's truck."

On another occasion he was with a group of fishermen having a 'yarn' on the seats at Little Hill, Port Isaac.

Will Avery pictured sitting in typical 'yarning' pose at Port Isaac Harbour. Will regularly exaggerated the size of his garden produce – a real character.
Courtesy of Stephen Found.   C 1937.

Will said, "One year grew a beetroot that big, ad to boil un in the copper."

One day, Percy May was having a 'yarn' with Will about gardening.

Will said, "One year teddies was that big, ad to dig um out with a crow bar."

One day, Tom Saundry, Bert Keat and a few other youngsters were walking down Port Gaverne Hill on the raised pathway, and Will Avery was walking up the hill carrying a basket of his potatoes. Will looked across at the boys and said, "There you are boys – look at that – no small ones amongst that lot."

Bert Keat walked over to Will and said, "Very nice Mr Avery." Bert then kicked the basket, and all the potatoes including the small ones which were in the bottom of the basket, went rolling down the hill. Perhaps I should add that I knew Bert Keat, and he was a gentleman.

Dick Oaten Also Boasted!

Many years ago Dick kept the small garden next to the Sight Cellar at Port Gaverne. He was there with Percy May one day digging potatoes, when Percy saw Dick picking out all the large ones and putting them in a bucket.

Dick said, "I'll show they b.....s down Little Hill."

Percy said that he went down to Little Hill, and told his mates he had dug them from only two stalks.

Tom Brown the Hairdresser!

For many years Tom was the local representative of Pawlyn's Fish Merchants of Mevagissey, and naturally he knew the fishermen very well, including my Grandfather Anthony 'Antny' Provis. Some local men occasionally cut their compatriot's hair, and on this particular occasion, Tom agreed to cut my grandfather's hair just before he was to be married. Tom started with the clippers at the base of the neck which was normal, but he then carried straight up over my grandfather's head, thereby leaving a bald furrow from his neck to his forehead. Of course, 'Granfer' wore a hat when he was married.

Have you Lived Here all your Life?

A visitor approached an elderly fisherman near the Platt, Port Isaac and said, "Have you lived at Port Isaac all your life?"

The fisherman said, "Not yet."

George Cowling and the Fox Skin.

The late George Cowling of Trelights always helped Bill Melhuish teal his potatoes in a field named South Park at Trelights. In return, George was allowed to keep one row for his family. Also he was allowed to set gin traps for rabbits.

One day George found a fox caught in a gin trap by its foot. He tried to approach the fox to free it, but each time the fox just snarled at him, so George decided it had to be killed, so he hit it on its head with a long handled Cornish shovel.

He then skinned it, and brought the skin plus the brush to his garden shed at Trelights, where he hung it on a nail on the shed door.

A couple of weeks later, Dick Cobbledick, who was a rep for Philp & Couch of Polzeath, called to collect an order for groceries. George showed him around his garden, and he offered to show Dick his fox skin which he intended to make into a fox stoll.

George opened the shed door and said, "Ere tis."

The skin then fell to the floor in a heap. George had forgotten to 'salt it down' before he hung it to dry, and the maggots had eaten the flesh. Dick Cobbledick couldn't stop laughing, and he told everyone on his round about it

John Sherratt Shouting for David.

John Sherratt was a son of George and Susie Sherratt, the village bakers, and John regularly called his son David in for dinner using his powerful voice. Each day during the school summer holidays, John knew that David would be on the beach playing with the rest of us, and regularly at about 12.55 pm, John looked over the Pentus wall and shouted incredibly loudly, 'DAVID'. Wherever we were on the beach, or even behind the breakwaters, we all heard the call, and of course it was also a timely call to us that it was dinner time. The call was a rather musical one, starting quite low with 'DA', and then increasing in pitch and loudness with the 'VID'. The 'VID' seemed to last some time, and whenever David heard it, he immediately stopped what he was doing, and ran up the beach, because he knew the call would be repeated until he appeared in view. Occasionally, if David was in the Pink Pool, or Giant's Rock area behind the Eastern Breakwater, he had a little distance to go before his father could see him, so the call was repeated until David appeared on the breakwater after frantically running over rocks and pools. Whatever David was doing, he stopped and sped off. If he was holding a stone, he dropped it; if we were in conversation, he just turned and ran. I sympathise with anyone standing next to John at the Pentus, but what happy memories.

Lizzie Couch Shouting for Richard.

I have been told that Lizzie Couch shouted in the same fashion for her son Richard from the Pentus. In this instance, the 'Rich' was shouted in a low note and the 'ard' was bellowed in a voice akin to a foghorn. Also similarly, Richard instantly obeyed the call. Goodness knows what sound John Sherratt and Lizzie would have made in unison!

Merle Asked Ray for Help!

Many years ago, Merle Arnold nee Honey was trying to start her car in Mayfield Road. She turned and turned the starting handle, but it still wouldn't start. She stood up exhausted, and saw Ray Provis just standing laughing at her. She said, "If you were a man you'd help me out!"

Ray said, "Well first of all, the engine's in the back!"

Selina Crocker.

Selina was a gypsy lady who visited Port Isaac during the late 1920s selling clothes pegs. Joan Dustow remembers residing in the Birdcage, Margaret's Lane, Port Isaac as a child, when Selina walked straight into her house, sat down and started smoking a pipe. Joan recalls moving around the furniture to get a better view of her, making Selina grin.

The Bradshaw Family, and the Itinerant Preacher.

Many years ago, an itinerant preacher stood on the Town Platt telling the locals how they were leading a bad life, and generally criticising them. Two members of the Bradshaw family, locally pronounced 'Braishall', took exception to this, and promptly forced the preacher into an empty fish barrel which was being kept on the Platt. They then gave the barrel a firm push down the beach with the unsuspecting preacher inside of it.

On another occasion, locals forced an itinerant preacher's head beneath one of the village pumps, and gave him a good soaking.

About ten years ago, a 50 year re-union organised by James Platt and his wife, was celebrated at the Temperance Hall during the day, and Port Isaac School during the evening for a meal and to reminisce. Those present left Port Isaac school about 60 years ago, and it is a sobering thought that only about half a dozen of those in the picture still reside in Port Isaac. I am sure they all consider themselves as 'Port Isaac people', even though circumstances have dictated they live elsewhere. James Platt is sitting in the front row wearing dark glasses with his wife alongside him. During the afternoon, Janet Chadband nee May supplied tea and refreshments.   *Courtesy of Merle Arnold nee Honey. C 2003*

Wet Paint.

A fisherman painted his boat 'black', and finished by painting on the boat in white, 'wet paint'.

From then on the local fishermen called the boat, 'Wet Paint'.

Words of Wisdom From Visitors.

Phil Tidy, a car park attendant at Port Isaac Beach was asked by a visitor, "Is the sea the same height at Port Isaac as Port Gaverne?"

Another visitor said to parking attendant Byron Buse, "They have ruined Port Isaac now. Last year we could park on the beach, now they have let the sea in."

Another visitor gave Byron £2 instead of £1 for parking on the beach. Byron pointed out the mistake and the visitor said, "Put the extra into getting the beach tarmacked for next year."

Before I explain the next incident, I must explain that all Port Isaac fishing boats are registered under the port of Padstow; hence their registered numbers all begin with PW.

I was on Port Isaac beach two years ago, when a visiting couple walked up to me and enquired if I was a local person, and I assured them I was. The lady then said to me, "Isn't it wonderful, they have even named the boats after Port Wenn!"

Jan Cowling was Related to Many at Trelights.

Jan moved to live at Wadebridge many years ago from Trelights, and a local there said to him, "Where you from boy?"

Jan said, "Trelights."

The local said, "You must be a Bunt, Browne or Cowling then."

Jan said, "Well, you're in luck, I'm all three!"

Clarence Smith and the Chamber Pot Money.

As a boy, Clarence lived in Chapel Street, Port Isaac, and when about nine or ten years old he did some odd jobs for Jimmy Vickery of Church Hill. One regular job was to empty Jimmy's chamber pot directly into the Lake. Clarence soon noticed that regularly 3d pieccs were appearing in the pot, as Jimmy kept his money under his mattress and during the night he would move and the money fell into the pot. Clarence gratefully collected this money from the Lake as a ha'penny then bought a large bag of sweets.

Port Isaac Community Celebrations.

This is another example of a small community reacting collectively to 'good news' stories, such as military victories abroad, or Royal weddings. This also shows how patriotic the Cornish were, although all Cornish were anxious to retain their local identity. The following account, plus the account of the celebrations of the new railway station at Port Isaac Road, must surely tell us something about the closeness of the community all those years ago.

Relief of the Siege of Ladysmith, Royal Cornwall Gazette, March 1900.

This was a prolonged engagement by the British Army during the Second Boar War. News of this victory was greeted with wild enthusiasm at Port Isaac as the following quote proves.

'Port Isaac was beside itself with joy. Very quickly the place bore a festival appearance, every available bit of bunting being spread to the breeze. A juvenile army, bearing numerous flags, paraded the streets, and nuts and sweets freely distributed among them. A monster bonfire was decided upon, and men and boys again and again toiled up a steep western height with broken fish boxes, tar barrels and pitch for a bonfire. At nightfall, piles were fired in various directions, blue lights burned, and several rockets sent up, while on the Town Platt there was a perfect fusillade from fowling places. Celebrations closed by the people proceeding en masse to the Coastguard Station, led by Mr H C Martin and others, and they gave round after round of lusty cheers for Queen and country, Army and Navy, and the several generals at the front. Then, as from one voice, came the national anthem'.

This is another example of a small community reacting as one to news of a military victory abroad in a very public manner. This account, plus the following account of the celebrations of the opening of the new railway station at Port Isaac Road, must surely tell us something about the closeness of the community all those years ago.

Opening of Port Isaac Road Station, Royal Cornwall Gazette, June 1895.

Formerly Port Isaac was reached by horse drawn coach from Wadebridge or Delabole, but on the opening of Port Isaac Road Railway Station on the 1st June 1895, access to the village was immediately improved, although the station was about three and a half miles from Port Isaac. The local community certainly knew how to celebrate this event as this very interesting quote from the Gazette proves.

'The fishing village of Port Isaac, which nestles in a cove, or as it is locally termed 'hawn', was en fete yesterday, the occasion being the extension of the North Cornwall Railway. The line from Wadebridge to Delabole has been constructed in the face of numerous difficulties. It is a great boon to the inhabitants of Port Isaac who happily know how to appreciate it. Yesterday's proceedings were most enthusiastic. Every house in the village displayed bunting, whilst rows of flags were across the streets, and at the entrance of the village was a triumphal arch with the word 'welcome' painted in large letters in cloth. The conveyances from the station to the village were also bedecked with flowers and flags. Fine weather prevailed, and the scene was most animated.

In the afternoon aquatic sports were held, and a fine dinner and tea were given the parishioners. A fine display of fireworks by Messrs Bearder & Sons, in the evening wound up the festivities. The Band of the 3rd DCLI discoursed an admirable programme under the direction of Bandmaster R Elford.

The event of the day was the presentation of an illuminated address to the Chairman, Mr Tremayne, and directors of the North Cornwall Railway from the inhabitants. Sir William Onslow - Bart, of St Tudy, represented the directors. Mr H Symons, JP; chairman of the Demonstration Committee, made the presentation, and in asking Sir William to accept it on behalf of the directors, expressed the pleasure it gave him to do so.

The address which was mounted on vellum, was exquisitely illuminated, reflecting considerable credit on the designer and executor, Mr H Williams, who also acted as secretary to the Demonstration Committee. On the border are three charming views; one of Port Isaac, another of a railway engine, and the third of a fleet of fishing boats. The address in an oak frame, the gift of Mr H Hills, stated that much satisfaction was derived from the fact that the place now stood within a comparatively convenient distance from the great iron track, and so had far better connection with the large centres of population. Its past remoteness had unquestionably hindered its expansion and progress, but 'well nigh' linked as it was now with the most popular system of intercommunication extant, there was a conviction that the prospects were there born to if not hitherto enjoyed. Through proximity to the London and South Western line the dispatch of fish for various markets would here-from be effected with greater convenience, speed and economy. Port Isaac would also be opened up more to tourist traffic, and so become better known for the salubrity of its climate, its romantic scenery, and other essentials for the making of a favourite holiday resort.

The Reverend Barclay acted as treasurer to the various committees, the members of which worked most energetically to make the day the huge success it undoubtedly was'.

So the locals welcomed the coming of the railway with open arms, but did they realise the devastating effect it would have on the slate trade of Port Gaverne, and the effect on the sailing vessel trade which employed so many local men? On the other hand, during the first five years of the railway arriving at Port Isaac Road, thousands of extra tons of herring and other fish, flowers, early daffodils and many rabbits were transported. Locally owned horse-drawn wagons serviced the station until the mid1920s. However, the old way of life, and Port Isaac's remoteness were altered irrevocably.

Celebrations Detailed in Volume Two.

For full details of celebrations at Port Isaac following the marriage of the Prince of Wales in 1863, and the arrival of the first Port Isaac wooden lifeboat in 1869, see volume two, 'The Seafarers of Port Isaac'.

Perhaps the most striking aspect of these celebrations was the huge community involvement, and the willingness of the locals to become totally involved with the excitement and atmosphere of the occasions.

It is said that World War One changed much in this country, and when one examines the patriotic faithful reaction to these 'good news' events, including war victories, I cannot help but think that the public's opinion of such matters changed after the horrendous loss of life suffered in that war. Perhaps the public were mainly dealing before this war with 'good news' stories about the glorious British Empire. I leave you to ponder this matter!

Small Photographic Collection of Community Celebrations.

This is a victory celebration at Port Isaac during the early years of the twentieth century, possibly after the First World War, but I cannot be sure. The people are dressed in the varying nationalities of the allies, and the close community celebrations involved are obvious.   Courtesy of Caroline Brogan-Taylor nee Provis.

The local Temperance movement march on Port Isaac beach early in the twentieth century. Note the banner on the left which appears to be a Band of Hope banner. Courtesy of Carol Brogan-Taylor nee Provis.   C 1910.

Children evacuated from a school in Brentford, Middlesex, appear in concert at Port Isaac in appreciation of their local foster parents. There may also be locals in this picture. Courtesy of Redruth Cornish Studies Library. 22nd December 1941.

The same concert by the evacuee children, and possibly some locals. Note the patriotic Union Jack flags. Courtesy of Redruth Cornish Studies Library. 22nd December 1941.

The cast of the same concert by the evacuee children, and possibly some locals.
Courtesy of Redruth Cornish Studies Library. 22nd December 1941.

The 'Wings For Victory' concert held at Port Isaac on the 26th May 1943. Note approximately twenty two
Port Isaac Boy's Brigade members near the back of the group wearing their distinctive hats. Note also
Mr Harold Spry second from the left at the back, and a young Jack Rowe standing at the back on the left.
In front of Jack is Maurice Brown, Michael Collings and Richard Couch. Further along is Fred Bate,
Ian Honey and Nick Bunt. The lady near the right of the picture with a white blouse is Yvonne Cleave nee
Leverton. For full details of the Boy's Brigade please, see the section on Port Isaac chapels later.
Courtesy of Redruth Cornish Studies Library. 26th May 1943.

A scene from the 'Wings For Victory' concert on the 26th May 1943. Note the war related posters at the back, and the various uniforms of the performers.
Courtesy of Redruth Cornish Studies Library. 26th May 1943.

Port Isaac Boy's Brigade provide a demonstration at the 'Wings For Victory' concert. Note the number of evacuees in the Boy's Brigade.
Back row left to right: Harold Spry, Capt; Norman Tansett, evacuee; Tim Scawen, George Wakeling, evacuee; Mark Prout, unknown, unknown, Ian Honey, Terry Selwood, evacuee.
Front row: Tony Gill, cousin of author; Eric Baker and Tony King, evacuees; Nick Bunt on stretcher and Fred Thompson, evacuee.
Courtesy of Redruth Cornish Studies Library. 26th May 1943.

A children's party at the Temperance Hall Port Isaac, organised by the Women's Royal Voluntary Service.
Note the children are eagerly anticipating their food! No doubt many evacuee children were present.
The fifth boy on the left is Dennis Collings, then Gerald Bedford and John Keat. Further on is a Hawkey
from Trelights.
The girl on the right smiling and looking at the camera is Barbara Honey.
Courtesy of Redruth Cornish Studies Library. 4th January 1944.

A Christmas party at the Temperance Hall organised for the Port Isaac elderly.
Second from the left appears to be Lizzie Couch.
Courtesy of Redruth Cornish Studies Library. 1949 or 1950.

Two elderly men enjoying the Christmas party at the Temperance Hall. I have been informed that the lady in the background between the two men is Gershal Hosking.
Courtesy of Redruth Cornish Studies Library. 1949 or 1950.

The cast of entertainers for the same Christmas party for the elderly people held at the Temperance Hall.
Back row from the left: These are male entertainers from various parts of North Cornwall. Third from the left is Jack Thomas, an accordion or concertina player from St Minver, and John Hicks appears to be at the end on the right partially hidden.
Front row from the left: Nora Keat, Roberta 'Bobbie' Derbyshire, Velma Knight nee Collings, Merle Arnold nee Honey, Veronica Keat, Diane Mitchell, Pearl Honey, Jean Sweet, Joy Collings in front; Josephine Provis, soloist, (the author's mother), and Mr Hillman the probable compere. The boy behind Nora Keat is Ernest Tucker, and the boy next to Josephine Provis is Tony Blake. The identity of the youngest girl in front is unknown.
Courtesy of Redruth Cornish Studies Library. 1949 or 1950.

Port Quin Social Life and Chapel.

Port Quin is situated 2.8 miles west of Port Isaac, and is a tiny village clustered around a rather narrow natural harbour. I dealt with the Port Quin disaster in volume two, but its history contains various periods when its population increased and then decreased depending on the availability of work and the prevalence of poverty. Four occasions when the population decreased are immediately apparent; the disaster in the seventeenth century when so many men were lost; the collapse of the pilchard fishing in the early nineteenth century; later in the nineteenth century when many people emigrated from Cornwall due to the general recession in the county, and again in the 1930s when a recession caused some families to move. Many Port Isaac families originate from Port Quin for the above reasons, as one option for people leaving Port Quin was to make the short journey to Port Isaac.

An aerial photo of Port Quin. Note the isolated nature of the village.
Courtesy of Jan Cowling.   Date unknown.

Whilst studying entertainment at Port Isaac, I wondered how the people who inhabited Port Quin many years ago entertained themselves, this being a small isolated village consisting only of a small number of labourer's cottages and a few larger houses. Several years ago I spoke to Cynthia Hutz nee Stone of Port Isaac whose Grandfather James Jasper lived at Port Quin, and farmed at Doyden Farm for Captain Connor, an ex-prison governor. James also kept the walled garden at Port Quin, and he grew vegetables for sale at Port Isaac which he transported by horse and cart. Cynthia's father was William Charles Stone, and he married Gertrude Jasper. At Port Quin, William was a fish jouster, and he also kept the 'middle watch' as a Coastguard at Kellan 'Look Out hut', starting at midnight. On marrying, he moved to a cottage in Fore Street Port Isaac which was nick-named 'Stoney's

Cottage', which then became 'Tinker's Cottage'. When Cynthia was four, she lived at 2 Dolphin Street, Port Isaac.

Cynthia's grandmother became ill, so she and her family returned to Port Quin to live, and Ray, Cynthia's brother walked to school at Port Isaac with other Port Quin children.

I asked Cynthia how the families entertained themselves, and her replies were both fascinating and enlightening. Perhaps it would benefit children today to read her account of life at Port Quin many years ago. She said there was no sewerage, running water or electricity, and candles or oil lamps were used. She confirmed that most people were not educated, but there was a strong community.

She said, "Mother always said it was the happiest days of her life living there, and Saturday nights were a real treat. Father used to walk to Port Isaac, collect the weekly newspapers, the post and sweets and stuff, and we would be bathed ready for him to come back from the trip, which was a real treat. Mother said that was her favourite day of the week, when he came back with the bits and pieces. When mother later moved to Port Isaac she often would say, 'I wish I could go back to Port Quin'."

I said, "Why was that?"

She said, "You see, it was a small community, and the people were all on the same plane if you know what I mean; people hadn't got up in the world then. Jim Cann was a farm labourer at Roscarrock Farm, and Mrs Keat had thirteen children. Women walked to Port Quin to buy cream off Mrs Tummon, and my grandfather let Jimmy Williams of Temple Bar have small potatoes for free. There wasn't much money around then, and they were all just making a living. Brother Ray and the Cann boys were devils, and they were always climbing around cliffs and valleys. When the gulls were nesting they went after their eggs, and once Ross Cann got trapped on a ledge near Kellan, and they had to lower a rope to haul him up. Douglas and Ross Cann once painted a pig with blue stripes, Charlie Keat

The Browne family of Trelights enjoying themselves at Port Quin in a wooden boat built by Reg Browne, a local Trelights carpenter.
Courtesy of Jan Cowling   C 1935.

was a 'stone waller' and it was all based on agriculture. There was no industry or fishing, but mother said it was the happiest days of her life."

I said, "I presume people helped each other out."

A super picture taken on the east side of Port Quin harbour at dusk. Note the narrow entrance. Courtesy of Jan Cowling.

The Roseveare family together with some locals enjoying an 'outing' to Port Quin by boat in either 1944 or 1945. They motored down to Port Quin from Port Isaac, but decided to row back to save fuel. Maybe there was a restriction on fuel because of World War Two.
Courtesy of Reuben Roseveare.   1945/46.

She said, "When Gran was bad, people came around to her with trays of tea and little treats. When my brother was born, Mrs Collins, Howard's mother, used to come around every afternoon with trays of tea and little things she had cooked to help grandfather. That was the community that was there. Groceries were delivered once a week, but everybody just walked to places. My father walked to Port Isaac to buy fish in maun baskets, and then he walked to Polzeath to sell it, but later he got a horse and cart. I remember old Mrs Tummon, a bent over old lady walking to church at Endellion; she was a big church lady. She also took her ducks onto the beach to feed on limpets; it was a wonderful life for children."

Cynthia said that her parents walked to St Endellion Church from Port Quin to get married at 8 am one morning, and returned to Port Quin in a 'pill box' or carriage.

I said, What about the Port Quin disaster which is talked about a lot?"

She said, "All I can tell you is that it was a legend to my grandfather, so it was a very long time ago. I heard there were memorial stones put at Endellion after the disaster, but I doubt it"

I said, "Howard Collins was a well known Port Quin man."

Cynthia said, "He was a wonderful man and swam a lot."

Finally, Cynthia said that the quickest way to walk to Port Quin was via Church Hill, through the hamlet of Lower Trefreock and over the fields, rather than the coastal pathway.

I dealt with the Port Quin disaster in my book, 'The Seafarers of Port Isaac', and I refer you to that. Also, at around the time of the General Strike in 1926, some families emigrated from Port Quin to British Columbia, Canada. Raymond Stone

Two Trelights ladies paddle in the waters at Port Quin.
Courtesy of Jan Cowling.   C 1935.

Jessie Roseveare sitting on the granite post at Port Quin, with Dorothy Oliver in the fore-ground.
Courtesy of Reuben Roseveare.   C 1935.

recalled that some descendants of those families visited Port Isaac, and inspected the old cottages at Port Quin once occupied by their ancestors.

Port Quin Men Helped the Coastguard.

A 'bad weather 'look out hut' was based on Kellan Head just east of Port Quin for many years. When the Port Isaac Coastguards attended an incident in the Port Quin area, some local men regularly attended to assist on the ropes, this being another example of close community involvement. Mr Dingle of Port Quin was regularly in attendance.

Port Quin Chapel.

Following the split in Methodism, the new Free Methodist Church wished to have freedom to choose their own lay preachers, but the Wesleyans continued as before. So in 1846, a new chapel was built and opened at Port Quin, but this has since either been demolished or simply fallen down, a fate which rather echoes that of historic Port Quin. Its location was as follows: Coming from the Long Cross direction, the road descends into Port Quin, and there is a sharp bend to the right at the bottom of this descent. The chapel was located about fifty yards up the hill from this bend, and over the eastern side hedge.

In the 1851 census, John Mabley reported there were seventy people in attendance at morning service, which seems an exceptionally good figure judging by the scattered population of the area and today's apathy towards religion. No doubt the people of Port Quin were joined by surrounding farmers, and perhaps by others from more distant villages. The chapel closed in the 1880s, so it lasted for about forty years, but I am sure the people of Port Quin greatly appreciated their little chapel. With general life being so hard, and poverty being common place, no doubt for the limited time the chapel existed, it performed a valuable service. However, I have no information about other chapel activities which are associated with similar establishments mentioned in this book.

Quay Cottage Port Quin. Take careful note of the rough ground and small trees behind the cottage. Mary Watts informed the author that this area contained old cottages in past days.
Courtesy of Cornwall Record Office.   C 1930.

Trelights Social Life and Chapels.

Trelights is a delightful small village situated in a naturally sheltered valley, and is 1.8 miles from Port Isaac, and 1.6 miles inland from Port Quin, which locals considered their beach. Polzeath Beach, being 4 miles distant was also popular for chapel 'outings', and the traditional local community consisted mainly of agricultural workers. My Great-Grandfather John Bate Mitchell was from a Port Gaverne seafaring family, but he could not work on the sea because of sea sickness, so he decided to work on the land, and he moved to Trelights where he raised his family. Joan Dustow informed me that he kept a garden adjacent to the hill leading to Trewithick, and when Joan was a little girl he called her a 'Little Lights Maid'.

Trelights has never possessed a pub or licensed premises, and the fair or circus did not visit. However, the close community organized their own entertainment, including various activities at the chapel and chapel Sunday school which was also their village hall, and dancing around the maypole behind Clemo's shop. There was a Post Office, a blacksmith and some small shops where people met and talked, but social activities were naturally very restricted. Nevertheless the locals were very content with life, although the usual poverty existed. Perhaps rather surprisingly, this small hamlet boasted a Bible Christian, and a Methodist Chapel.

In contrast to the above rather sedate description, during the smuggling days, a roomy cellar in a garden at Trelights was used for the storage of contraband. However, given the widespread nature of smuggling, this was not altogether surprising.

Originally Trelights consisted of two villages, Trelights and Trewithick, but the two now converge.

Port Quin – Their Beach.

These are perhaps the most remarkable 'outings' mentioned in this book. During the summer months of the 1930s and possibly before, the local ladies organized summer 'outings' to Port Quin. This was not a chapel initiative, and there was no particular person in charge of this, as the small population all knew each other, and ideas were quickly passed around from one to another. The 'outing' consisted of the grandmothers, mothers and children of Trelights, all walking the 1.5 miles to Port Quin, and then spending the day on the beach before walking back to Trelights. Cafés did not exist at Port Quin, so refreshments were carried by the ladies. The beach is very narrow, consisting of rocks and stones with only some sand at low water.

The caves and shoreline at Port Quin were explored thoroughly, and they learned that the cave on the right as you look out to sea at Port Quin contained a room hacked out of the rock which was used by smugglers. They were told that to access this room, one had to take a ladder into the cave, and climb to reach it. Another cave on the left as you look out to sea contained an adit, which was probably made for extracting antimony ore, which is quite common in the area.

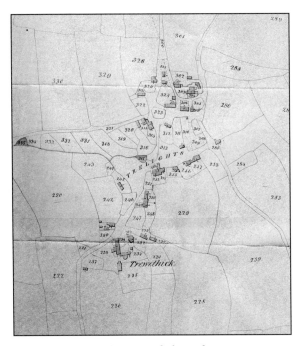

The 1840 tithe map showing Trelights and
Trewithick as separate villages.
Courtesy of Jan Cowling.

Reg Browne of Trelights on the left
fishing at Port Quin. Note the quaint
fishing rod. The gentleman on the
right is not known.
Courtesy of Jan Cowling.   C 1935.

Roger Worth, aged three, playing outside
of his grandfather's smithy at Trelights.
The Trelights youngsters grew up in
natural surroundings, and Roger was
making the most of the family business.
In fact he still resides in a house
connected with his family.
Courtesy of Roger Worth.   August 1938.

A photo of Trelights taken in 2013
showing the rural setting of the village with the sea and Port Quin 1.6
miles distant. There has been some
expansion in recent years, and some
of the residences are hidden as they
are in a shallow valley.
Photo by Geoff Provis and taken
from the garden of Graham & Kay
Strout nee Byfield.

My immediate reaction when I heard of these activities was, 'what pure uncomplicated pleasure'. The men worked whilst these 'outings' occurred.

During school holidays, and sometimes after walking home from Port Isaac School, the children walked or cycled to Port Quin which they also considered their beach. Occasionally they walked through the valley to reach the beach where they learned to swim in the rock pools and the caves, and played on the sand if the tide was out. If it was an 'all day' visit, then packed lunches were taken. On shorter trips the children walked home very hungry, and occasionally a turnip was taken from a field to eat, but they always arrived home hungry.

'Kiddleywinks'.

As stated, there were no pubs at Trelights, but a house there nicknamed 'Kiddleywinks' was used by the men folk to drink alcohol, but it was not licensed. My understanding is that it was rather a 'laid back' affair, in keeping with the general character of Trelights.

Travelling Cinema.

During the 1950s an old lorry occasionally parked outside of the Post Office, and the children sat on the road and watched the films being projected from the back of the lorry. Regular viewers were David Chapman, Irene and Ann Chadband, Peter Blake, Jan Cowling and sister, Susan Jones and David Dingle.

Maypole Dancing.

Each year the children danced around the Maypole in a field behind Clemo's shop. Trelights did not have its own carnival, but occasionally a Trelight's float entered the Port Isaac carnival.

Celebration of the Coronation at Trelights.

The following newspaper report, kindly loaned to me by Jan Cowling comments on the Trelights celebrations of the Coronation of Queen Elizabeth the Second in 1952, but I do not have the name of the paper.

'Trelights, unlike most villages, had no village green until it was decided to clear, fill in and level what used to be an old pond. This effort, in which almost everyone in the village took part, made it possible to hold a very impressive ceremony on a gaily decorated site to celebrate the Coronation.

After prayers for the Queen, and a short address by the Rev RB Scurrah, a copper beech tree, (the gift of Mr and Mrs Keatley), was planted by Mrs J Cowling and Mr J Morrish, the two oldest inhabitants. Mrs Morrish was afterwards presented with a bouquet by Miss Pam Hawkey.

Mr LT Strout of the Parish and Rural District Councils in a short address, commended the spirit and effort shown, and asked for further support to make and keep the green permanent. Three other trees, gifts of Mr H Kent and Mr Marshall Blake, were also planted.

Mr E Bunt, an 'old boy' of the village, presented souvenir mugs to the children, and called on the two youngest schoolboys, M Dingle and J Smallwood, to hand the gifts to the old folk.

The Browne family below Quay Cottage, Port Quin. From the left: Doreen Browne, Millie Browne and Peggy Browne. The small girl is Joy Browne, and Reg Browne second from the right. The man on the right is unknown.
Courtesy of Jan Cowling.   C 1931.

Trelights ladies and children on an 'outing' to Port Quin.
Courtesy of Jan Cowling.   C 1935.

This very ordinary looking house at Trelights, now named 'Hillside', was originally nicknamed 'Kiddleywinks' by local people. As there was no pub at Trelights, it was used by locals to consume alcohol although it did not have any licence.
Photo taken by Geoff Provis   2012.

This wonderful photo was taken in 1909 on Polzeath beach during an 'outing', possibly a chapel outing from Trelights. Transport was horse and cart, and they invariably stayed on the western or Tristram side of the beach. This photo includes members of the Cowling, Bunt, Browne and Bishop families, and the photo has the feel of a traditional seaside 'outing'. You will also note that all were related. Contrary to today, the centre of the beach was left empty.
Back left: Harry Bunt, Blacksmith of Trelights; Jenny Browne nee Bishop; Lillian Browne nee Keat holding Jack Bishop; Harry Browne, carpenter, son of Richard; Nellie Bunt nee Browne; Richard Gill Browne, Great-Grandfather of Jan Cowling.
Middle left: Charles Bishop, son of Jennie; Mab Bishop, mother-in-law of Jennie Bishop; Elizabeth Browne, wife of Richard Gill Browne.
Front left: Nancy Bishop, sister to Jack Charles & Guy; Rita Cowling nee Bunt, step mother to Jan Cowling and Guy Bishop.
Courtesy of Jan Cowling.   C 1909.

Although Trelights did not have their own carnival, occasionally they entered a float into the Port Isaac Carnival as above.

Rear from the left: Fred Hawkey the jockey on horse; Roy Mitchell's wife, ?, ?, Bill Worth the bookmaker and Roy Mitchell the rich horse owner.

Front left is Dorothy Lane, Millie Worth nee Bunt; Betty or Beryl Blake, Rita Cowling nee Bunt; a Browne girl and possibly Doris.

Courtesy of Jan Cowling.   C 1950.

Trelights children. From the left: Donald Strout, Gwen Strout, Joan Dustow, Joyce Melhuish and Bet. Dingle.

Courstesy of Jan Cowling.   Early 1930s

Tea, presided over by Mrs M Blake and helpers, was followed by a sports meeting, at which the races were keenly contested.

The evening was spent at the chapel hall with more games for the children, songs and music by young and older entertainers, and the presentation of sports prizes by Mrs RL Browne'.

The following details relate mainly to the chapels and their various activities. These, and the coronation celebrations explain in detail the close community spirit in Trelights in days gone by, when people naturally made their own fun.

Trelights Bible Christian Chapel.

The rather small unpretentious dwelling named 'Chapel Villa' at Trelights was at one time the Bible Christian Chapel, and its history is very interesting. How Christianity was brought to such places during times of horse transport and no modern communication is quite inspiring, and the individuals concerned must surely have conveyed their religious convictions in a forthright and persistent manner. A female minister Betsy Reed brought the Bible Christian form of Methodism to the general area in 1818, this being the year the first 'meeting' was established. The first Bible Christian Society at Trelights is dated at 1820, when two of Betsy's converts, Nicholas Carveth and Thomas Hawke began to meet with others. Hawke lived at Trelights, becoming a local preacher and dying in 1878/79.

A native of Port Isaac, Richard P Tabb, born in 1802 and whose parents were Wesleyan Methodist, was the Bible Christian President of Conference in 1848, and he was converted at Trelights. The following is an extract from his autobiography. 'About 1819, I made known to my parents the desire I felt to be a Christian. I met with a friend, a young man who had joined not long before, the Bible Christian Society at a village called Trelights. He took me to a class meeting, and for the first time in my life I was found in a Methodist Class Meeting, where the Lord's people spoke most freely out of full and glad hearts of what the Lord had done to their souls. I heard in that fellowship meeting the way of the Lord as I had never heard it before. I gave myself to God and poured out my heart before him. Light more and more, broke in upon my soul'.

Tabb became a member at Trelights and a local preacher, and at the age

'Chapel Villa', Trelights, which was originally the Bible Christian chapel. Photo by Geoff Provis. 2013.

of 26 he was called into the ministry. The actual Bible Christian Chapel at Trelights was opened in 1837, possibly 11th June, and it was described as a stone walled slate roofed building.

In the 1851 Religious Census, the evening congregation was 80, and this underlines the importance of the chapel. Perhaps I should add a word of caution here, because churches and chapels made a special effort to ensure good attendances for this census, however, this should not detract from the importance of the chapels to the local communities. My only local information about this chapel is that 'fiery preachers' attended services there.

The Bible Christian movement was started in 1815 by William O'Bryan, and they were known informally as 'Bryanites'. Based in the West Country, the Bible Christians were allied to the working classes and agricultural labourers, whereas the Wesleyans were favoured by the small landowners, merchants and business people. Another difference was that Wesleyan Ministers attended training college, but Bible Christian Ministers were simply judged by their performance at work

The Bible Christian Magazine of January 1844 states: 'Thank the Lord for another day. What a mercy to enjoy good health, and above all the favour of God. A Blessed meeting this evening at Trelights in the parish of St Endellion. In our society in this place we have several truly devoted to God who feel deeply interested in the Missionary cause. The collection; £1.6s which was a trifle above last year; besides a young female in this place last year, collected £2'.

Trelights Bible Christian 'Missionary Society' Donations.

The following are some details of collections made at Trelights Bible Christian Chapel.

1879.	£2.16s.6d.	Mrs Bolt, 'a friend', Mrs Hawke, (card), Miss Brown, (box).
1882.	£2.2s.	Mrs Hawke, (box).
1883.	£1.10s.	Mrs Hawken, (box).
1884	£1.1s.3d	Miss May, (box).
1885	£1.11s	Miss Brown, (box).
1887	£1.18s	- do -
1888	£1.18s.8d	-do-
1890	££1.9s.9d	-do-
1892	£3.4s.9d	Miss Cowling, (box).
1893	£3.7s.11d	Miss N Brown, (box), self denial meeting.
1895	£1.9s.3d	Miss A Jones, (box).
1896	£2.2.2d	Miss H Jones, (box).
1897	£2.9s	Miss Kate Cowling, (box).
1898	£2.7s.4d	Misses Mary and Ann Hewitt, (box).

By 1898, the Bible Christians boasted a mission in China, and also funds were being raised towards a hospital in Yunnan. Trelights gave £2.6s.1d towards this during a visit by the Rev F J Dymond. Mr Jones of Trelights was present at that meeting.

1899   £2.7s.3d   Misses Mary and Annie Hewitt, (box).
1900   £1.16s.9d   -do-

At Porthleven, which boasted a Bible Christian and a Wesleyan Chapel, the Bible Christian collections named actual fishing vessels, and certain amounts collected aboard the vessels; thus the chapel was referred to there as the 'Fishermen's Chapel'.

In 1907, the Bible Christians united with two other groups - see later. In the St Austell clay strike of 1913, former Bible Christians supported the strikers, and a former United Methodist Free Churches minister gave active support with picketing.

Trelights Bible Christian Chapel in 1904.

Sunday services were held at 2.30 and 6 pm, and 7.30 pm fortnightly in May and June. The chapel anniversary was the 15th May. The same preacher conducted both Sunday services. No local preacher or auxiliary hailed from Trelights, and the society stewards were Bro Cowling and Miss Roseveare. The chapel was not licensed for marriages.

Amongst the more interesting collections made at the chapel were for the 'worn-out preachers' fund'; 'horse hire collection' and the 'lighting collection'. An interesting point is that 'Horse Hire Collections' were made up until 1932, many years after most travel with horses had ceased. This cash was simply paid into their specific fund to subsidise their travel.

'Exhorters' for the circuit were the Boscastle Mission Band.

Closure of the Bible Christian Chapel.

In 1907, the United Methodist Free Churches, the Bible Christians and the Methodist New Connection united into the United Methodist Church. In 1909-10, the Trelights Bible Christian Chapel closed and worship continued at the ex-United Methodist Free Churches Chapel at Trelights.

Finally, the Bible Christians always allowed female ministers.

Trelights Methodist Chapel.

Of the five chapels discussed in this book, this chapel thankfully is the only one surviving as a practicing place of worship, and a current chapel stalwart is Peter Blake, who is anxious to maintain its tradition. The previous chapel began life in 1831 as Wesleyan in the old Camelford Circuit, and was paid for by public subscription whereby the public were able to buy shares. This meant that if the chapel made a profit, the subscribers were able to receive a dividend, thus its 'deed' was irregular by Wesleyan standards.

The first Wesleyan society existed in the village from 1822, apparently with a chapel, but that lapsed. However, in 1826, a permanent society was established. In 1835 the annual Wesleyan Conference expelled several ministers over contentions about a theological training college, and this caused grievances in various parts of the country. At the same time at Camelford, there were local schisms, and the Trelights congregation found themselves in sympathy with the objectors, so Trelights also became part of the new Wesleyan Methodist Association. The irregular Deed mentioned above, meant that the Wesleyans could not re-claim the Trelights Chapel.

Photo taken outside Trelights Methodist Chapel of the wedding of Susan Jones of Trelights and Gary Gettings of Delabole. Many people decided to marry at St Endellion Church, however Susan and Garry utilised the Methodist Chapel. Their eighty guests crammed into the chapel, and part of the Sunday school was used to accommodate the overflow.
Courtesy of Jan Cowling and Susan Gettings nee Jones.   Date 29th August 1970.

In 1857, the Wesleyan Methodist Association Camelford Circuit joined the newly created United Methodist Free Churches.

In 1887, the Trelights Chapel was re-built or renewed, and I give details of this as follows:

Laying of Memorial Stones for a New Methodist Chapel.

On the 13th August 1886, the Royal Cornwall Gazette reported as follows: 'Memorial stones of a new chapel for the use of the Methodist Free Church at Trelights in the Camelford and Wadebridge Circuit, were laid on Friday by Mrs Coleman of Rock Hill, Mrs Guy of Park Villa, Mrs Edwards of Trebelthick, St Mabyn, and Mrs Stephens of Tor View Camelford. Tea given by Mr and Mrs Guy, was provided in the grounds of Park Villa.

An open air meeting in the evening was held, the service commenced with singing and prayer, the latter being led by the Rev R Percival. A portion of scripture was read by Mr RM Oliver, and an address on the history and policy of Methodism was delivered by the Rev J Cleave'.

New Methodist Chapel at Trelights.

The Royal Cornwall Gazette of 8th August 1887 covered the opening of the chapel as follows:

'A new chapel for the use of the United Free Methodist Church at Trelights near Port Isaac was opened on Thursday. The service commenced with singing and prayer, the latter being led by the Rev R Percival. A portion of scripture was read by

Mr HM Oliver, and an address on the history and policy of Methodism was delivered by the Rev J Cleave. The Rev H Williams, a returned missionary from Sierra Leone preached in the afternoon. A bazaar was afterwards opened, and a public tea provided in a field near the chapel. In the evening, the Rev W Skinner presided over a public meeting which was addressed by the Revs H Williams, J Bentley and Mr HM Oliver. The society has succeeded in raising nearly the whole of the debt, being only £30'.

I deliberately include the above details as they show the dedication of the small village to have their chapel, and how much it meant to them. The number of activities connected with the chapel again demonstrates its value to the small local community.

This small active chapel, still has its Sunday school room, and over the years this has been used for business, local council meetings as well as harvest festivals,

Members attending Trelights Methodist Chapel. Long may it 'buck the trend', and continue to serve the community. Nearest the camera is Barbara Richards nee Finnemore; Bryan Richards with his back to the camera; the shorter man is Charles Symons and the lady in the doorway is Elaine Found nee Short.
Courtesy of Clarinda Truscott nee Blake.   C 1980.

anniversaries and chapel teas where the children were permitted to have one split only, and one piece of Mrs Gynn's rich dark fruit cake. Horatio Clemo of Trelights usually sang solo at such events, and suitable recitations and holy songs were sung. When primroses were in season, the children walked to Pinehaven to pick them to decorate the chapel. Pinehaven, the cove just west of Port Isaac, is about two miles from Trelights, and their route was mainly across fields. Surely this effort by the children tells us something about the social nature of the village. No doubt in 2013, parents would not be happy to allow their children such freedom, even if the children were prepared to do it.

Garden Fete for the Methodist Chapel.

The following newspaper cutting giving details of a fund raising effort to raise money for new heating and lighting at Trelights for their chapel. I do not have the date, but it would have been between August 1936 and August 1940, as this was the period the Rev Hewitt was in this particular circuit. Again, I include what may seem to some a rather mundane report, to show the importance of the chapel to a small hamlet or village. The comparison between the efforts to raise funds, and the closure of many hundreds of similar establishments during these secular days is depressing for any Christian.

'Trelights, the little hamlet situated midway between St Minver and Port Isaac was the venue of many Methodists and others on Wednesday week, when parties from Tredrizzick, Port Isaac, Polzeath and Wadebridge gathered to support the effort of the local Methodist Church to raise funds for the proposed heating, and electrical lighting of the chapel and Sunday school.

Four boys pictured outside of Trelights Sunday School: From the rear left: Roger Worth and Brian Blake. Front from the left: Bill Chadband and Colin Mitchell. Note, the boys are dressed in their 'Sunday best'. Courtesy of Roger Worth.   C 1948.

Flags and streamers floating in the breeze attracted the visitors to 'The Laburnams', the residence of Mr and Mrs Ivey, for the garden fete held on the lawn in front of the house.

Rev HR Hewitt, (Port Isaac), minister in charge of the Camelford and Wadebridge Circuit, as chairman, was supported by Mr W Symons, Wadebridge Circuit Steward.

The proceedings commenced with the hymn, 'Summer Suns are Glowing', fully proved by the brilliant sunshine that afternoon.

The opening ceremony by Mr and Mrs Wilkinson of Windmill, St Minver, was short and appropriate, their remarks being rewarded by the presentation of a buttonhole, and a well filled basket of fruit by the two young daughters of Mr Browne.

The afternoon was devoted to the 'fun of the fair', every available spot having something to 'bring grist to the mill'. Mr Goodfellow and Mr Chapman took charge of the gate, the entrance fees adding considerably to the day's results. Mesdames H Dyer and Burt had the supervision of the work and fancy stall; Mrs C Symons and Miss Dyer, under the shade of the garden arch dispensed ice cream and sweets; flowers, plants and vegetables were well displayed by Miss Ivey, (winner of several awards at the recent Port Isaac flower show); and Miss Hall and Miss Joyce Thomas had charge of the fish pond and dip.

Games for prizes were well patronized, those assisting being Messrs W Colwill, W Goodfellow, G Hawken, C Ivey and C Symons. The prizes were won by Mr R Bishop, a section of honey for pegging the line; Mr Melhuish, a duck for darts; Mr Stapleton a chicken for skittles; Mr Gordon Tilsley a pig for howling; and Mr E Abbott a chicken for bagatelle.

For the tea arrangements those responsible included Mesdammes W Colwill, J Kent, Miss Kent and Mr Croft. Visitors in the district whose services were much appreciated, provided the programme for the evening concert under the chairmanship of the Rev Hewitt, being: violin, Miss Priscilla Hoskin Port Isaac; cello, Mr Parkinson; solos, Miss Leamon; duets, Master H Symons and D Collings; recitations, Miss Welch and Master H Symons. Mrs Hoskin accompanied throughout.

The net proceeds of the garden fete amounted to £24. 5s'.

An excellent wedding photo taken outside of the old Post Office at Trelights. It features members of the Lobb family of Port Isaac and Trelights.
Front row from the left Rev. Scurrah, the non- conformist minister, then Beatrice Provis nee Lobb, the author's great-grandmother and auntie of the bride. The gentleman sitting next to the end of the front row with a white beard is Richard Lobb, my great-grandmother's brother who resided at Trelights. One of his daughters Ellen Irene Lobb was marrying a New Zealand serviceman. The boy sitting on the ground is Roy Deer.
The gentleman fourth from the right in the back row is Guy Hawken of Port Isaac, and his wife is at the end on the right. Between them is Mr and Mrs Deer who originally owned the Post Office. The ladies in white are either sisters or cousins of the bride.
Provis family photo – courtesy of Harold Provis.   C 1917.

Horatio Clemo.

Horatio was well known both at Port Isaac and his home village of Trelights for his excellent voice and musical prowess. The following extract is taken from a Trethosa, (St Austell Circuit), booklet dated 1976: 'Amongst the most notable singers who have been in the choir at Trethosa is Mr Horatio Clemo, who formed a young people's choir known as the 'The Harmonic Choir'. He later made a distinguished career for himself in New Zealand, where his musical talents were greatly appreciated. In retirement he returned to live at Trelights where his widow still resides'.

Horatio, or 'Raish' as he was named locally, organized concert parties annually which were based at Trelights Chapel. These usually consisted of a male vocal quartet consisting of Harold Spry of Port Isaac; Roy Dingle of Trelights; Mr Cocks of Rock and himself. The Blake twins, Beryl and Betty formed a vocal duet with one another, or a Brown girl from St Endellion. John Clemo, Horatio's son, and Roger Worth formed a comedy duo with Roger playing the 'straight guy'.

Roger Worth recalls performing with these at Burlawn and Tredrizzick Chapels, as well as others during the early 1950s. Both children and adults were involved.

Trelights Drama Group.

This group was part of the Methodist Chapel, and the Sunday school room was used for plays and rehearsals. This was a winter activity, and very much a village venture. The Sunday school boasted a small stage, and therefore it resembled a village hall although it was small. Rita Croft played piano and prepared costumes, and Mrs Browne worked on the scenery.

Trelights Methodist Chapel Guild and Youth Club.

The Guild consisted of a youth club attached to the chapel, and Rita Cowling was the organizer. Competitions were held with other chapels, and there were different sections to the Guild covering, recitation, singing, horticulture and playing musical instruments. During horticulture, the children made gardens out of biscuit tins, and Police Constable Bearne of Port Isaac gave first aid lectures to the children during the late 1950s and early 1960s.

Occasionally Trelights boys walked to Port Isaac to visit St Peter's Youth Club in the Church Rooms.

Current chapel stalwarts include Barbara Richards nee Finnemore, Joan Murray nee Honey and Peter Blake, and no doubt without such people, this small chapel would not be surviving today.

Methodist Chapel 'Outings'.

The furthest 'outing' was to Paignton and Torquay, and during days of horse travel, Polzeath was the favourite destination.

Jan Cowling recalled that as a young boy he forgot to take his bathing costume to St Ives on an 'outing', so he was given a pair of ladies briefs to wear.

Pendoggett Social Life and Chapels.

Pendoggett is a very small village bordering three parishes; St Endellion, St Kew and St Teath, but due to it being only 2.5 miles from Port Isaac, I am including it in this book. The number of houses in the village has varied over the years, but a figure of around fifteen or sixteen should give the reader an idea of the size. In olden days, the area by the pub was known as 'Up Town', and the area around the chapel as 'Overtown'. Two large farms nearby tended to increase the local population as Treharrock Farm contained between six to eight houses, and Treore Farm about three or four, and the farmworkers who occupied them obviously provided children for the chapel and Sunday school. In a
similar manner to many Cornish towns and villages, the chapel played an important role in its social fabric, however, I commence with the manner in which Pendoggett locals enjoyed themselves in 'days gone by'.

As a further preamble, Pendoggett Garage, Post Office, Co-op, Chapel, Sunday school, shop, carpenter's shop, public reading room, blacksmith and village hall have all now closed, these being ideal places for locals to 'drop in' for a 'yarn' or to entertain themselves.

Entertainment at Pendoggett.

The population of Pendoggett was always small, and the people made their own entertainment with their chapel at the centre of village life. At the end of the 6 pm Sunday service, especially during the summer months, the families enjoyed a

A photo taken outside of Pendoggett Post Office during the 1930s.
From the left: Tom and Mary Cowling, (Tom was the local carpenter). Edith Cowling, their daughter,
later to be Edith Wearne plus a visitor.
Courtesy of Win Leverton.   C 1935.

Another photo of Pendoggett Post Office. Written on the back of the photo is, 'in the good old days'.

From the left: a visitor, Edith Wearne nee Cowling, and 'Tren' Rush, (real name Ellen Trenarry Rush nee Cleave). Mrs Wearne lived in the house to the left of the post office. The black door was the entrance to the shop. The door on the right was a 'holiday' let.
Courtesy of Win Leverton.
C 1955.

'Tren' Rush closing and locking the old Pendoggett Post Office door for the last time in 1966. 'Tren' was a Cleave from Dinnabroad. The Post Office business moved a little way up the road to the small shop opposite the Cornish Arms pub.
Courtesy of Win Leverton.
1966.

country walk before going home for tea. A typical walk was the road towards St Endellion, and then turning left towards St Kew on Gravlins Lane, and then back to Pendoggett on the St Kew Road. These walks enabled the people, some of whom had travelled from outlying areas, to converse and enjoy interacting with each other.

The Old Post Office.

Miss Edith Cowling was the postmistress, and the Post Office consisted of a small shop where groceries and paraffin were available if you could find them. Chickens regularly walked in and out of the doors, and old glass cabinets were scattered around the shop full of bits and pieces. An old cat and dog regularly patrolled inside the shop, and Jessie Trayes 'Aunt Jessie', often sat in the shop with her old clothes on.

A visitor, Mr Gazzard serving himself with petrol from the pumps which were outside of the old Pendoggett Post Office. The pumps were worked manually.
Courtesy of Win Leverton. 1953.

Barbara Richards nee Finnemore said, "Couldn't see her unless she moved!"

Two manual petrol pumps were outside the shop and operated by Edith who later became Mrs Wearne. The Post Office counter had no shield, this being the only counter in the shop.

Jack Gill's shop opposite the Cornish Arms. To make the shop pay, Jack operated a 'country round'. Fred Malloy continued operating it after Fred. Courtesy of Marion Mewton.

Two goats were sometimes tethered up outside the shop, and on one occasion Bill Finnemore's horse panicked on passing the goats, and it pulled his trap up past the pub when a cyclist stopped and grabbed the horse around its neck and stopped it. Terry Gifford recalled when he was a small boy living at Port Isaac, he heard that Miss Cowling had 'tops' for sale, so he and his mates walked to Pendoggett hoping to buy some, but she had sold out. In 1966, the old Post Office finally closed.

The Cornish Arms and Attached Shop.

The Cornish Arms existed, but many of the locals did not believe in drinking alcohol due to their Methodist leanings. A small shop was attached to the Pub, adjacent the garage, and Gwen Hooper remembers two sisters named Beare were the proprietors. They sold sweets, clothes and other oddments. This shop then became a branch of the Co-op, and was under the control of Mrs Mickelborough, the only person who worked there from 9am to5 pm each week day. Mr Auger of the St Teath branch was in overall charge. The Beare sisters moved to Trelights where they ran a haberdashery shop. Jack Gill later opened a shop opposite the pub after the Co-op closed.

Fred Neil's Garage.

Fred Neil's Garage was on the site of the later Mewton's Garage, and he charged batteries and accumulators, made and repaired bicycles and sold petrol during World War Two. The original garage consisted of concrete blocks and a tin roof, and the land for building it was purchased off of Pendoggett Farm for £50, the field in which it was located being named Mitters Field, and the only one on the farm consisting mainly of clay. A very small shop was attached to the garage, and a number of dart boards were kept there for use of the locals and visiting teams from neighbouring villages for competitive darts matches. It was also used for a meeting place to play

John Goodfellow initially acquired Fred Neil's garage, but after a relatively short period, Edward Mewton purchased it in 1952. This photo shows the garage in the process of being modernised by him. Edward is standing outside immediately to the left of the petrol pump.
Courtesy of Marion Mewton.

cards during the day and evening. Fred Neil also delivered milk fresh from his farm at Lane End, Pendoggett, and provided a taxi service to Port Isaac Road Station. Gwen Hooper recalled that Fred was very deaf, until he eventually had his ears syringed, and from that time on he could not stand noise.

Edward Mewton's Garage.

Edward acquired the garage in 1952 from John Goodfellow who in turn had acquired it off of Fred Neil, but for only a short period. Edward modernized it and he repaired cars, operated a taxi service to Port Isaac Road Station, sold petrol, paraffin, accumulators, radio batteries and tobacco. Claude Cann delivered Sunday papers to the garage which locals found very useful. The garage was purely then operated as a business, and there were no dart boards or card games etc. However, locals found Edward and all the staff there very personable and friendly. In 1984 the garage business at Pendoggett ceased.

Public Reading Room.

Across the road from the garage was an old railway carriage which was adapted for use as a public reading room. Newspapers and magazines were placed there, and it all was

The Cornish Arms Pendoggett with Mewton's Garage petrol pumps just visible to the right when they had been moved to alongside the main road. I do not deal with the history of the pub in this book.
Courtesy of Stephen Found. 1960s.

bought by public subscription, again a good example of the locals jointly acting to provide for the community. Later this carriage was used as a 'cow shed' by Tommy Chapman after its original use ceased.

The Cowling family carpenter's shop was situated on the main road, and no doubt this was also a local meeting place.

Tommy and John Sherratt of the Port Isaac Bakery delivered their goods by means of a van, and once a week a Prout's bus from Port Isaac conveyed the ladies to Wadebridge to do their shopping, after dropping off other passengers at Port Isaac Road Station. The bus returned in the early evening. Once a fortnight a van from Wadebridge Co-op visited the village and it also sold cigarettes.

Terry Gifford described the people of Pendoggett as being 'a very nice little community'. They certainly made their own fun through what may be considered today as simple community activities. Terry's father played the concertina, and during the Second World War people held parties to keep spirits up. They just came to the parties and sang and had fun. Apart from Port Isaac and Port Gaverne, travel was essential to reach the seaside or any centre of population, but they were very happy with their lot. Gwen Hooper walked with her friend to Port Isaac, two and a half miles, and Delabole, four miles, to attend dances.

She said, "Everybody was so friendly. At Christmas, some houses held parties, and three or four times a year parties were held in the chapel hall. The chapel was really the centre of everything. It was lovely living at Pendoggett, we all knew everybody and everybody got together to do things."

Pendoggett Village Hall.

In 1948, Henry Hawken the licensee of the local pub gave land for the village hall to be built at Lane End, Pendoggett. Dick Thyer erected the blocks and helped with the floor, and a tin roof was again used. This served as a village hall for many years after the Second World War. (Lane End is the lane roughly opposite the Pub). On Monday nights, Basil and Mary Cleave held dancing classes there, and I recall as a youngster walking from Port Isaac with some mates to 'check out' this activity. Mrs Mickelborough operated a 'wind up' gramophone for the dances, and during one night she asked Ken Finnemore to operate it for her whilst she took her dog outside. Ken broke a spring in it, so he had to go to borrow one off of Edwina Billing of Higher Hendra.

On six Wednesday nights during the spring, the Beare family organised whist drives at the hall. When the track leading to the hall became pot holed, a truck brought ashes from Port Isaac Road Station to fill in the holes.

Concerts and birthday parties were held in the hall, and such acts as the Goonhavern Banjo Band, the Pedlar Brothers from Lockingate, a conjuror named Mike Nicholls from Trewalder ; concert parties from St Breward and the Mallet Concert Party from St Neot all performed there.

Tren Rush and Mrs Mickleborough organized Christmas parties there, but when a young Roger Stone met his first Father Christmas there, he recognized his voice

Football Field.

The pub owned a seven acre field across the road from its location, and Pendoggett men occasionally raised a team to play St Kew as a local challenge. Also Delabole CP School and St Kew CP School played six-a-side games there. The goal posts were 'home made', or coats and jumpers used.

Days Spent in a Signal Box.

Peter Chapman recalls being 'dropped off' at Port Isaac Road Station by his father during the early 1960s when he was six or seven years of age. He then spent the days in the signal box watching the trains and with some effort, pulling the heavy levers.

Private Museum.

James Henry Hawken, a Pendoggett character and magistrate, kept a private museum near his house at Pendoggett. He allowed local children to enter and see the exhibits which they fully appreciated. The museum was at the end of the buildings containing Cowling's carpenter's shop. It contained artifacts he brought back from Africa including stuffed animals, spears, bows and arrows and a large xylophone. Later these artifacts were acquired by the Truro County Museum.

Guy Fawkes Night Celebrations.

During the 1940s and 1950s, Graham Tom the father of Henry, regularly gave Howard Crahart £10 to buy fireworks at St Lawrence's Fair Bodmin. The fire was lit on the 'top field' which was located on the Treore Road on very high ground. This was visible for miles around, and people came from quite a wide area to join the celebrations.

It is worthy of note, that the comparatively wealthy Tom family were continuing to be very 'community minded'.

Visits of Boy Scouts from London.

Les Salmon was a Second World War evacuee at Pendoggett, and he was associated with the scouts in London. Later he returned with a group of scouts on an annual basis, and they regularly sat around a fire in Jack Hawken's field and enjoyed a 'sing song'.

Port Gaverne - Their Beach.

Gwen Hooper recalls during the late1930s and 40s walking with her family to Port Gaverne from Pendoggett to spend time on the beach.

She said, "That was our seaside place."

She said they all mounted a stile at Pendoggett, and continued on down Port Gaverne Valley on a footpath, and came out near Trewetha where they cut down over the hill to Port Gaverne. Food was carried such as pasties, and after an enjoyable day they walked back to Pendoggett, a distance of two and a half miles. Other Pendoggett families also enjoyed Port Gaverne in this fashion.

Pendoggett House.

During the 1930s and the early Second World War, Miss Jennings kept Pendoggett House as a guest house, catering for about eight or nine persons on a 'full board' basis. This was the only guest house at Pendoggett, and she employed various local people in the house and also in her gardens and two fields. The house also boasted a tennis court. Colin Gifford milked her two or three cows, and drove her to church at St Kew every Sunday morning in her pony and jingle. Her clientele usually returned year after year.

When Eileen Gifford worked a 'half day', she often collected her younger brother Terry in the pony and trap, and took him to Port Gaverne Beach, tying the pony up outside of Bertha's Café.

Pendoggett House is the first house on the left when entering Pendoggett from the St Endellion direction.

Whilst reading how Pendoggett people entertained themselves in days gone by, it is obvious that it was a far less technical age, when locals obtained full satisfaction from indulging in straightforward activities. Transport was less available, so the people made the best of their situation and made their own 'home entertainments'. However, many things changed in 1939 at the start of World War Two. Whether or not this change was as great as that which occurred after the First World War is in doubt, but the war changed the habits and customs of Pendoggett.

The original Pendoggett Chapel built as far as we know in 1829. This later became the Sunday School on completion of the later chapel. It is very small, and I was surprised at its appearance, the exterior being quite original.
Courtesy of Tony Gabriel, the owner.
Photo by Geoff Provis.   2013.

The replacement chapel built at Pendoggett to replace the small old one. This is now a dwelling, a fate suffered by many such buildings.
Photo by Geoff Provis.   2013.

Pendoggett Chapels.

The first 'cottage meetings' at Pendoggett date from 1804, and the first chapel from 1829. (TS).

The Tom family of Treharrock Manor, were instrumental in the building of this chapel, which was constructed in 1897 in place of the inadequate older chapel. The following is the story as told by Gladys Tom, the daughter of Henry Tom who is the 'father' in the story below.

'When father and mother came to Treharrock, they found there was a poor little building in the village down in a hollow behind some cottages. It was a damp dismal building with a wheezy harmonium in it, and it belonged to the United Methodist Free Church denomination, and was very badly attended. Father and mother used to go to Port Isaac Wesleyan Chapel as they were Wesleyan, and at Port Isaac there was a big

Henry Tom, the man responsible for the building of the second Pendoggett Chapel as told by Gladys Tom. Although it was Henry's initiative to build the chapel, locals worked hard to pay off the debt. Courtesy of Juliet Cleave nee Tom.

chapel, a good organ well played, and a splendid choir, but I think their consciences bothered them a bit.

Gwen, Kathleen and Leonard used to go daily to Trefreock, a farm near Port Isaac, where a Mrs Pascoe assisted by some other teachers had quite a good school with several boarders as well as day pupils. One morning, Leonard was taken very ill there, and was unconscious. Mrs Pascoe thought he was dead, so she sent a man on a horse galloping to Treharrock for father and mother, and another was sent to Port Isaac for the doctor.

When father and mother arrived at the school, they both also thought the child was dead, but mother took him, put him in a warm bath and held him there keeping the water as warm as she could, and massaging his heart. Father stayed downstairs

The interior of the second and last chapel at Pendoggett. Courtesy of Barbara Richards nee Finnemore.   C 1960.

and prayed. He made a promise during a prayer that if his son's life was spared, he would build a new chapel at Pendoggett. The child regained consciousness and recovered, and they set about building the chapel, buying a piece of land, and the village men and others gave their labour to make the foundation, and helped the masons and carpenters, with much of the work being voluntary. The little chapel was built with a stable and trap house, (in which was a copper to boil water for public teas), for the Minister's and preacher's horses and traps. The old building was kept and father started a Sunday school there, and there were about 60 children attending it'.

Stone Laying & Concert at Treharrock for New Pendoggett Chapel.

A newspaper report dated 19th July 1894 gives details of the stone laying. Stones were laid by Misses Gwennie and Kathleen Tom; Miss Hill, Hayle; Miss Gertrude Edwards and Doctor R Julyan George, Port Isaac; and in the name of the Sunday school by Miss Bessie Thomas.

A concert was held at Treharrock after and the following artists performed: Delabole Brass Band, Mrs Parsons, Port Isaac – soloist; Mr Parsons, Port Isaac, violin; Miss Edwards and George – piano pieces; Mr & Mrs Hawke, Delabole, duet; Miss Hooper, soloist and Mr H Symons gave a recitation.

UMFC Festival at Pendoggett. Royal Cornwall Gazette 14th June 1900.

'About five years ago, a neat and substantial little chapel was built at Pendoggett near Port Isaac in connection with the United Methodist Free Church. The trustees were saddled with a considerable debt which the chapel members endeavored by special effort to extinguish'.

Although Henry Tom played a large role in the building of this chapel, it is obvious from this newspaper article that a debt was incurred which the parishioners worked hard to settle. It is possible that Henry assisted with the finances, but I have no information about that.

Pendoggett Chapel Sunday School.

The old chapel building was renovated at the same time as the new chapel was built. Henry Tom organised a Sunday school there with about sixty children attending, assisted by Mr Withy Hill, and they acted as superintendents on alternate Sundays. Two men and two ladies were recruited to take the Sunday school classes, and the four classes were taken in the same room with the high backed pews used to divide the classes. The superintendent sat in the pulpit to oversee matters. Each Christmas the children in the school who had attended six times received a book as a prize, and this was presented after the morning service on Christmas day.

Mrs Tom taught the children new tunes for Sunday school anniversaries, and most of them had something new to wear, and everyone had a button hole of flowers. After anniversary services in the afternoon and evening, the children had free teas, sitting on the two trestle tables in the Sunday School. The water was carried in galvanized pails from the well at the bottom of the lane beneath the Sunday School, and boiled in a copper in the Trap House. Four ladies brought their own teapots and

Pendoggett Sunday school members showing off the main shield for the Camelford and District Youth Festival. Christine Beare and Barbara Finnemore performed as a duet and were never beaten. Mrs Priscilla Milne taught piano and the pianist was Mrs Marjorie Beare.
Back row from the left: Colin Cleave, Allan Finnemore, Bill Cleave, Christine Beare, Margaret Beare, Barbara Finnemore, Margaret Hawken, Barbara Prout, Theresa Bates and Pauline Beare.
Front row from the left: Mary Warne, Sheila Finnemore, Carol Lobb, Bill Finnemore, Sunday school superintendent; John Mewton, Peter Bates and Tom Warne.
Courtesy of Barbara Richards nee Finnemore.   1955.

china and made the tea. The teapots were placed at each end of the tables, and there were two sittings with Grace being said before each sitting.

Sunday School 'Outings' to Polzeath.

Gladys Tom continues her story, and describes in graphic detail an 'outing' to Polzeath during the time of horse travel: 'Once a year we used to take the children and their parents, and anyone who liked to go, for an 'outing' to Polzeath. The farmers lent their wagons, and fitted them up with planks for seats, and then decorated them with branches. Each wagon had two horses to pull it, and they held about twenty people. The whole village except for two or three old people turned out for this, the only outing of the year. Everybody took their own mid-day meal, usually pasties, and had family picnics on the beach or cliffs. We organized games on the beach for the children, and they paddled in the sea, with always someone falling in and getting soaking wet. All gathered for tea on the sand bank by the old Post Office, which was then the only shop in Polzeath.

Jack Crahart used to make a fire with a tripod, and hang fountains, (like an iron tea urn), which hung under the steps of the waggonette which was filled with water coming from the spring on the right side of the beach. We fixed trestle tables and cut bread and butter, splits with jam and cream, saffron yeast cakes, buns, and also a rich fruit cake. We all then sat down and were waited on by the teachers. Every day seemed fine for the 'outings'.

The Gifford family of Pendoggett on a Sunday afternoon outing to Polzeath.
Boys at the rear from the left: Ronald, Colin and Aubrey Gifford.
Front from the left: Marjorie Gifford, later Donnithorne; Florrie Gifford, Ernest Gifford, Ruby Gifford
and Bill Kent. The baby in the front is Terry Gifford.
Courtesy of Terry Gifford.   C 1934.

The horses were tied to the wagon wheels after being unharnessed, and given nose bags. During the day they were taken down to the water to wash their legs in the salt water'.

This is an historic account of an 'outing', and of considerable interest. My only comment is, that the Tom family were quite well off financially in comparison to average locals, so no doubt they ensured there was an abundance of food.

Gwen Hooper said that much later during the 1930s and 1940s, Prout's bus of Port Isaac was hired once a year to take the chapel children to West Cornwall after the chapel anniversary.

Barbara Richards nee Finnemore said that during the 1950s, 'outings' were made to Perranporth, St Ives, Looe and Westward Ho, and Fry's coaches of Tintagel eventually took over from Prout's of Port Isaac. Sunday school children attended these 'outings' free of charge, and guest children paid.

Pendoggett (Port Isaac), United Methodist Free Church Band of Hope.

The following report of their festival appeared in the Royal Cornwall Gazette in May 1899:

'The Pendoggett (Port Isaac) UMFC Band of Hope had a successful festival on Thursday. After the tea, which was well patronised, a Temperance meeting was held, Mr Mark Guy of Port Gaverne presiding. Messrs W Symons and Cleave were the principal speakers. The choir sang several pieces, and Delabole Brass Band assisted'.

It was considered a great honour at Pendoggett to be allowed to carry the flags and banners as they processed through the small village. Two or three stalls were always in attendance on these days, selling sweets, sherbet and small toys and the children happily spent their pennies on these items.

Sunday School Anniversaries in the 1940s and 1950s.

Horatio Clemo of Trelights, an excellent singer, trained the chapel choir after Easter until the anniversary in June. Other good singers travelled to these practices to take part such as Mr Boundy from St Teath, Les Prout, Mr Hawke and Mr Richards from Delabole, and Claude Prout from St Breward. Mrs Wearne nee Cowling was the organist, but she did not like anyone else playing it. Sunday school superintendent was Bill Finnemore.

Cakes and teas for the anniversary teas were supplied by Radcliff's of Delabole. Following the teas, sports were held in the field next to the chapel consisting of racing, egg and spoon races and three legged races.

Chapel Guild.

Tuesday nights were 'guild nights'. The guild consisted of meetings at the Sunday School, where such social events as quizzes, teas and speakers were enjoyed. Many people attended who did not normally attend the chapel.

A chapel coffee morning held to raise funds for the chapel in a garage opposite the chapel just across the road from the chapel itself. Unfortunately, it would soon be closed. From the left: Howard Crahart, Gladys Finnemore nee Crahart, Dorothy Tucker, Bob Cleave and ? Courtesy of Win Leverton nee Cleave. Early 1980s.

The wedding of Clifford Warne and Elizabeth Chapman at Pendoggett Chapel 14th February 1942.
Back row from the left: Samual Wearne, Stanley Harris, best man; Percy Chapman, Mavis Chapman, and Tom Chapman.
Front row from the left: Ivy Warne nee Harris; Clifford Warne, bridebroom; Elizabeth Warne nee Chapman, bride; Hilda Chapman nee Hambly and Gran Hambly. Picture taken outside the cottage attached to the Cornish Arms Pendoggett.
Courtesy of Tom and Sandra Warne.   1942.

Bazaars.

Two bazaars per year were held in the Sunday School; one in the spring and one in the autumn. Sometimes Mrs Wearne allowed a bazaar to be held in her garage. Ken Finnemore remembers wrapping presents and then putting them in a tub of sawdust so that people had to fumble around in the dust to retrieve their presents.

Concerts.

Usually two concerts were held per year in the Sunday School. Chapel stalwarts included Howard Crahart, Tom Hill of Penquite, Henry Tom of Penhill and the Wellington family of Pennytinney.

Harvest Festivals.

These were held once a year in October, and the chapel was appropriately decorated with the usual produce. Following this, the produce was conveyed to the Sunday School and auctioned during the evening with Howard Crahart and Eldred Beare being the auctioneers during the 1950s.

Services in a Field.

In the summer, on fine Sunday afternoons, a small group of chapel members with a portable harmonium went to a small field to sing hymns and pray. Mrs Tom played the harmonium, but there were no sermons. Some people who never attended chapel attended these services, and later many of these joined the chapel.

Such events would be unthinkable in 2013, but they do tell us something about the importance of religion to small communities during the early 20th century.

Pendoggett Village Choir.

Mrs Henry Tom attended boarding school at Mecklenberg House, Putney, and there she learned piano and harp, and received singing lessons. She later trained Pendoggett Village Choir, and taught them their parts, even though none of the members could read music. The village carpenter, Robert Cowling had a wonderful voice, but he could not read, so he often sang notes as 'SOO – SAA'. One verse of a hymn ended, 'At thy feet I bow', but Robert's version was, 'soo saa, bow wow now'.

Nick Hambly, a 'real old' Pendoggett character. Nick regularly drank in the Cornish Arms, and visitors continually bought him drinks whilst he sat on his regular stool, so he always arrived back home 'tight'. He had various jobs such as farming and a council roadman, being responsible for a stretch of road from Pendoggett to St Endellion and beyond.
Courtesy of Tom and Sandra Warne.   Early 1990s.

Funerals at Pendoggett.

Pendoggett does not have a burial ground, so traditionally families walked to Amble behind the hearse carried on a wagon, a distance of 4.4 miles. Trelill Chapel burial ground has also been used on occasions, a distance of 2.2 miles.

Conclusion.

A real vibrant small local community existed at Pendoggett for very many years, but I am afraid that community was another victim of progress and secularization in the twentieth century. What a shame that we cannot progress without destroying such things!

Port Gaverne.

Port Gaverne, the near neighbour of Port Isaac has been described as 'the natural playground of the two places with its pleasant beach, rocks, caves and boating, and what is the only really safe bathing cove along the coast'. However, it has always been in the shadow of Port Isaac, although it has its own character and distinct history. Geologically it is similar to Port Isaac and Port Quin, being also a flooded valley. The construction of four large pilchard cellars at around 1800, and the export of slate from Delabole increased its importance. In relation to 'entertainment', Port Gaverne's clean and safe bathing beach was, and is its main attraction. The Port Gaverne Hotel was extremely popular with sailors in the days of sail, and no doubt some sailors who had endured a hard voyage bringing coal from Wales, or materials from further afield, indulged themselves with a 'well earned' drink. The vessels were unloaded on the beach after the tide receded, so the 'turnaround' time was very slow, especially as another cargo, usually slate had to be loaded, giving the crew ample time to socialize if they could afford to do so.

Following the demise of the slate and sailing ship trade, Port Gaverne gradually became very popular with holiday makers and locals alike, for its natural beauty and relatively safe waters.

I asked four ex-Port Gaverne residents their opinions of 'old' Port Gaverne.

Bessie Selway.

Bessie remembered living at the Port Gaverne Hotel between 1920 and 1928; her father John Selway being the proprietor, having bought the hotel off of Mr and Mrs Charlie Keat. John married Ann Bishop born 1878, the daughter of Mark Bishop, and she previously worked in the hotel on the catering side. He dropped the hotel license and it became a private hotel selling teas, cigarettes, pottery and mineral waters. However, if people wanted alcoholic drinks, he brought them from the Golden Lion pub at Port Isaac. At this time Jack and Bertha Mitchell rented a cottage attached to the hotel, but as John needed the room, he asked them to leave. Harry Hills of Port Isaac

A.C.U.

PORT GAVERN Private Hotel,

PORT ISAAC,
NORTH CORNWALL

THIS comfortable Hotel is situated within twenty yards of the safest bathing sands on this coast, and is surrounded by magnificent cliffs and scenery.

BOATING   FISHING   BATHING
DANCING
A modern equipped Dance-room - - with Maple Floor - -
LIBERAL TABLES   BEST ENGLISH FARE
ACCOMMODATION FOR MOTORISTS
GARAGE
LUNCHEONS AND TEAS PROVIDED TO NON-RESIDENTS

Moderate Tariff

Proprietor—JOHN SELWAY

An advert for the Port Gaverne Hotel published in 1927 whilst under the ownership of John Selway. Note a maple dance floor was mentioned. 1927.

A very good picture of Port Gaverne showing the Headlands Hotel suitably painted in black, probably during World War Two, the premises being used to house evacuees. Courtesy of Olive Strout nee Honey.   C 1943.

A good photo of Port Gaverne Hotel in years 'gone by'. Courtesy of Malcolm McCarthy.   C 1920

An interesting photo showing the bathing huts at Port Gaverne and Mitchell's Tea Rooms on the right. The Port Gaverne Hotel and Pink Cottage are clearly visible. Courtesy of Olive Strout nee Honey.   C 1935.

worked on the hotel, and he built the top windows. Bedrooms were built over the stables, which were separated from the hotel by a cob wall.

People came from as far as St Tudy by horse and wagon, stabling their horses behind the hotel, and then enjoying the teas and scenery, however, the hotel was sold in 1929 to Peter Calverly for £2,000.

Bessie said that local children often took potatoes to the lime kiln to cook them in the hot ashes.

She said that although the population of Port Gaverne was very small, it was usually quite busy 'in season', with people from Port Isaac coming to use the beach which was much cleaner than theirs, which was polluted with sewage. People from Pendoggett and the surrounding area thought of Port Gaverne as their beach, and they occasionally made daily walking 'outings' there during favourable weather. Three beach huts located at the top of the beach, below what is now a small car park were owned by Mrs Elizabeth Honey, Joey's wife, and later by Bertha Strout. Bertha did not like salt or sand in the huts, so she asked users to rinse off in the leat on the beach. There was no general transport available to go to Polzeath, which was a special treat reserved for Sunday school 'outings'.

Bessie remembered Joey Honey living in a cottage to the right of the lime kiln when a serious kitchen fire occurred in the cottage. All the local Port Gaverne inhabitants helped put the fire out using buckets of water taken from a pump, which was just to the right of the kipper house. The helpers were paid half a crown for their efforts. Joey later moved across the stream to his cottage attached to a large cellar, which he also owned.

Charlie Mallet, a Frenchman and fisherman, and the father of Theresa Lobb and Bessie Couch, lived in a house attached to the kipper house cellar and he went fishing with Joey Honey. Billy Brown, a fisherman, lived in a cottage next to the Green Door, and next to him was Mark Bishop.

I explain these details to show the nature of the inhabitants of Port Gaverne during times 'gone by'.

George May informed me that a small sweet shop was attached to the corner of 'Bide-a-While, and he regularly stopped

Theresa Lobb nee Mallet, who I knew well in her older years, carries a pale of water to her cottage at Port Gaverne. A clear demonstration of the slow yet hard way of life at Port Gaverne many years ago. The cottage was previously part of a pilchard cellar. Courtesy of Olive Strout nee Honey. C1925.

98

Bathers modestly dressed enjoying their swim alongside the moored fishing boats at Port Gaverne.
Courtesy of Juliet Cleave nee Tom.   C 1935.

Port Gaverne fishermen sitting on the seat which has been in situation for many years. Another evocative
photograph displaying the true character of Port Gaverne.
From the left: Charlie Mallet, a shipwrecked Frenchman who settled in Port Isaac and Port Gaverne, and
who married a local lady; Mark
Bishop, Jack Taylor, Captain Maskell, a retired captain from outside the area who lived on The Terrace;
unknown, Billy Brown and unknown.
Courtesy of Janet Chadband nee May.   C 1935.

there whilst walking to Brooklands Farm which is on the path towards Port Gaverne valley on the eastern side of the stream.

Percy May.

Percy was born in 1925, and at the age of two he moved with his family from Church Hill, Port Isaac to Brooklands Farm, Port Gaverne Valley. Percy said that until the move, his family attended the Wesley Chapel Sunday school, but this stopped after the move. I asked him what he did for entertainment growing up at Port Gaverne. He said that all he remembered doing was working; the girls worked indoors, and he and his brothers outdoors on the 30 acre family farm.

Percy said that he remembered there were only three families at Port Gaverne when he was small, Jack and Bertha Strout nee Mitchell, Joey Honey and family and his own. He said that Charlie Mallett was still living, but he died while Percy was still young. Percy said that when the Price family moved into Port Gaverne, people were on their best behaviour when dealing with them, as they employed several locals. Perhaps another 'sign of the times', as locals were glad of any work during the early twentieth century.

Joey Honey, a real Port Gaverne character pictured with his dog 'Fluff'. He grew his own tobacco using seaweed as fertiliser. He hung the leaves in his cellar to dry, and pressed them using his own 'self made' press. He named his tobacco 'PGP' short for 'Port Gaverne Plug'. The tobacco was for his personal use, and the clouds of smoke emitting from his cellar tended to support this theory. Mr Bramble, a retired bank manager helped Joey with his fishing, and Jimmy Creighton of Port Isaac who kept a garden near Bide–a–While, and my father Cyril Provis, also shared the tobacco at times.
Courtesy of Olive Strout nee Honey. C 1945.

Les Mitchell.

In past years, Port Gaverne's population was even less than Port Quin's, and I asked Les Mitchell, a local man now living in New Zealand, to explain about his childhood at Port Gaverne during the 1940s and 50s:

'Moving to Port Gaverne at the age of seven was a bit of a shock, as Cousin Bob Strout who was four years older, and Brian Orchard, who was also seven, were the only other kids there. There were refugees at 'Bide a While', whom we only saw at, or walking home from school. The beach and valley were our favourite playgrounds, although I do remember riding with Percy May down Headlands Hill on an old Fordson tractor, and holding on for dear life. Another playground was the area where the boats 'laid up' by the lime kiln, but they were big, and not easy to climb aboard for a seven year old. The *Winifred, Our Boys* and *King Eddy* spring to mind, with the *Boy Will, Kate,* and the *Dawn* among others in the cellar under cover.

Mitchell's Tea Rooms built in about 1911 by Idabella Mitchell. Actually built by Taylor's of Port Isaac.
Courtesy of Olive Strout nee Honey.   C   1920.

A very young Bob Strout playing in the fish cellars at Port Gaverne. Later he would explore the beach and valley with his local mates.
Courtesy of Olive Strout nee Honey.   C 1938.

A nice photo taken outside Mitchell's Tea Rooms Port Gaverne.
From the left: Wendy Holland nee Hicks; Linda Honey nee Sherratt, Bertha Strout nee Mitchell
and Jack Strout the café owners.
Courtesy of Olive Strout nee Honey.   *C 1962.*

The Port Gaverne Valley occupied us kids during the school holidays, at Christmas, and at Easter when we built huts in the 'Great Wood' and bridges over the stream. (To reach the 'Great Wood', walk past Brooklands Farm for a little way, cross a bridge to the other side of the valley and the 'Great Wood' was a short distance from the stream). In the autumn, picking blackberries, hazelnuts, and occasionally mushrooms was the order of the day. Summertime was spent on the beach, swimming at Teague's Pit, and playing with tin boats beaten out from the biggest tin you could find. (Teague's Pit is the small inlet near low water on the east side of the beach). When I was older, I helped with the dinghys rented to visitors by Joey Honey, assisted by Mr Bramble, a retired bank manager. They were joined later by 'little' Jim Sweet with his dinghy. As you would know, mackerel fishing was also popular after work on fine summer evenings'.

Les of course took part in many activities later at Port Isaac, and I give details of these later in this book. After completing his apprenticeship with Harold Donnithorne, Les joined the RAF for two years national service. I shall let Les continue:

'There were no shops in Port Gaverne, only the tea rooms during the summer which sold cream teas, baskets for picnics on the beach, soft drinks, sweets, chocolates, after rationing and cigarettes. In winter, cigarettes could be bought at 'The Rockies' in Port Gaverne Hill.

Groceries came from the Co-op in New Road, Chapman's of Fore Street, and meat from Hicks's of New Road or Worden's of Middle Street, Port Isaac. We bought our groceries from Philip Couch of Polzeath, Jack Cobbledick calling on a Tuesday to collect the order, and Jim Davey delivering the groceries on the following Friday. Jim was a good footballer and played for Port Isaac.

In 1942 Mrs Calverley was the licensee of the Port Gaverne Hotel which was a popular 'watering hole' for Polish Airmen at Davidstowe, and later the Canadian and American Servicemen. At the end of World War Two, Mrs Calverley left the hotel and converted the ground floor of the Venus Cellars into the Green Door Club.

After demob, I found a lot of things had changed in a very short time. People had left the village or had died, and a lot of the cottages had been bought by strangers. Many of my own group had left the village in search of work, and the village had a different feel about it which is hard to put into words'.

His letter to me makes his affection for Port Gaverne and Port Isaac quite obvious, and his comments about the sale of cottages, and locals moving away for work based on the situation between 1945 and 1958 were accurate then, and indeed prophetic, as the situation in 2013 proves.

Les is a Cornish Bard; see section on Port Isaac Social Life.

Annie Price.

Annie is the grand- daughter of Lady Gurtrude Price or 'Gurty' and Sir Keith Price. In 1905 'Gurty' and her sister -in-law Dorothy decided to cycle from Surrey to Cornwall. They ended up in Port Gaverne and spotted the Port Gaverne Hotel. They fell in love with a derelict cottage next to the hotel named Atlantic Cottage and initially they rented it. In 1908 they purchased it off H Bate for £250 for use as a holiday home. They used the well by Pilchard's Corner which is near the Lime Kiln, and collected milk using pails from Trewetha Farm. Fishermen brought mackerel to the cottage each day when in season, and they cooked them on a wood burning raeburn in the cottage they named ' Mother Hubbard'.

Lady Price also bought Pilchard's Corner Cottage and Beach House from the Guy family, plus the fish cellars next to Beach House. She was good hearted and wanted to make life easier for the fishermen and avoid them having to pay rent for use of the beach, so she bought the foreshore at Port Gaverne to protect them. The following locals worked for the Prices: Annie Brown looked after the cottage in the old days; Jim May Snr dug the back garden; Tom Couch did the washing and Betty Couch the cooking. At one stage, Joey Honey was also the gardener of Pink Cottage. Fishing boats were kept on the front lawn of Pink Cottage.

In 1952, Lady Price decided to give all her Port Gaverne property to the National Trust except for Pink Cottage, and one garage behind Pilchard's which remains in the Price family.

The Price family went out fishing with Joey Honey, and on one occasion one of them felt sick. Joey told the person that he or she could be sick in his boat as they may hurt their neck reaching out over the boat!!

To conclude, I am very grateful to Bessie, Annie, Les and Percy for sharing their memories of Port Gaverne with me.

A fascinating photograph loaned to me by Gordon Keat. It shows a procession of horse drawn carts slowly making its way up Fore Street, Port Isaac. The carts are full of goods which suggests they are destined for a market or fair of some sort, perhaps Ollacombe Fair. If so, these people may be travelling sales people or 'tinkers'. Ollacombe Fair was held in a field nearer the top of the village. Just looking at the photo, gives us an idea of the importance of such occasions.
Courtesy of Gordon Keat.   C 1900.

Port Isaac Social Life.

In the olden days the population of Port Isaac made their own entertainment and social life, as the village was very isolated indeed, with transport being very rudimentary before the development of the motor car. Also many families struggled to get enough food, so this basic need was often accompanied by an enjoyable method of achieving the same result. To study the ways in which the local community responded to hardship, and also times of celebration, throws an illuminating light on the true nature of the community, and how families played and worshipped together. Indeed some reactions to 'good news' stories do appear rather extreme, as is demonstrated by the reaction of the village following news of the relief of the Siege of Ladysmith. To demonstrate to the reader the various ways the community lived and played, I give examples of those varied activities so that the reader may have a clear picture of the nature of the village, and the close community spirit.

On occasions fishermen took family and friends on pleasure trips in their boats. On this occasion William Harris Steer Snr did just this in the DARING, a 22'6" vessel.
Back row from the left: Lewis Cann and William Harris Steer Snr.
Middle row: Tom Strout, stranger, stranger, William Harris Steer Jnr, Kathleen Steer, Lewis Cann's wife, stranger, stranger and Edith Steer.
Front: Ruby Steer and the young boy - William Harris Steer Jnr.
Courtesy of Bill Steer. C 1932.

Men caught rabbits for sport, and returned with enough rabbits to give away to grateful residents, and to provide a nourishing meal for their families. They also engaged in 'bird beating', and caught enough song birds to make 'birdie pie', as well as having enjoyed the process of catching the birds. Concerts were arranged to pay for a local nurse prior to the Health Service, so here again the concert provided enjoyment, as well as paying for an essential service. Following sea tragedies in the nineteenth century when numerous family men were drowned, special concerts were held, and the proceeds were given to the widows, sometimes in the form of hundredweights of coal, and details of these are in volume two. Games were played by the local youth, many of which are now forgotten. The old Port Isaac wooden gigs were also used for racing against gigs from Padstow and Newquay, as well as performing their traditional role. Occasionally, Port Isaac fishermen raced their fishing luggers against Padstow and Newquay luggers. The village paid particular attention to lifeboat practices and launches, news of military victories abroad, the opening of Port Isaac Road Railway Station, and certain Royal celebrations brought the community together in an impressive manner. In fact it is interesting to compare the enthusiastic manner in which the very poor villagers in days gone by celebrated such matters, with the more muted celebrations of today. Was life so hard then, that any reason to come together as a community was seized upon enthusiastically to provide some brief relief from the harsh realities of life, or was the community then so much closer than modern day communities, they having to work hard together to survive? I find it impossible to compare the 'old' Port Isaac with that of 2013, where so many properties are effectively empty, being used as holiday homes or second homes. Some streets are almost 100% empty for a proportion of the year, which were filled with mainly Cornish people in my youth. I have spoken to long term visitors, who for many years have visited Port Isaac, and they have explained to me how appalled they are that the Port Isaac they knew and loved does not now exist. By saying this, I am not in any way criticizing the people both local, and those who have moved here from other cultures, who are making efforts to establish a new community.

Men gathered at the same meeting places in the village to tell stories about literally anything, and the importance of these gatherings in cementing together the old village should not be under-estimated. I do not apologise for repeating the details of this in my books, as scenes of men 'yarning' at various places in the village, defined the nature of the village in past days. The Port Isaac carnival was a very popular event, and travelling fairs and traction engines with their brass work gleaming visited the village. Numerous events were associated with the chapels and churches, such as 'outings', harvest festivals, Boys' Brigade, Band of Hope, Wesleyan Guild, garden fetes and various parades, choirs and tea parties. Port Isaac had its own cinema the 'Rivoli', Temperance Hall, Church Rooms, a cottage which acted as a sports centre; Working Men's Club, Old Cornwall Society, British Legion, 'Ollacombe' Fair, wrestling or 'wrasslin' tournaments; football, badminton and tennis clubs, a boys football club, more latterly a cricket club; choral society, harmonica quartet and many other organisations, the vast majority of which do not now exist. Indeed, some of the above are not recorded officially anywhere, and I have come across them almost by accident.

Port Isaac School was used during its early days for social meetings. Therefore this section of the book will deal with a large number of different topics all associated with entertainment.

All of the above activities helped to bind the community together during times of poverty and hardship, and helped to give the village its unique character.

An example of village interaction was as follows. After chapel on a fine Sunday afternoon, the youngsters occasionally went walking, perhaps to Port Gaverne or up one of the valleys. Sometimes a boy or girl lost contact with the main bunch, and that was the first sign that they were courting.

The following is a list of activities and games associated with old Port Isaac. I do not pretend that it is in any way complete, but I hope there is sufficient information for you to gain an appreciation of the manner in which the village entertained itself many years ago.

Holy Thursday Fair, 'Hollycome' or 'Ollacombe Fair'.

Fairs visited Port Isaac at other times of the year, but the favourite fair and the one most talked about was 'Ollacombe' Fair which was of course once a year. I have been asked before the meaning of 'Ollacombe', and Bessie Selway informed me that it is the local derivation or version of 'Holy Come'. As 'Ollacombe' is Port Isaac slang, the spelling of this word will vary. From at least the mid-nineteenth century and for some time before, this was a most important event. The three days of 'Ollacombe' were on Holy Thursday, Friday and Saturday. The following quote from the Royal Cornwall Gazette of the 18th May 1893 makes interesting reading:

'The 'Hollycombe' as Port Isaac Feast was called, was held on Thursday, Friday and Saturday – not on a Sunday as generally is the case in other places. The rough 'past times', games and drinking bouts of a past generation have disappeared, and it may be said to be kept more in the breach than in the observance'.

So the 'Ollacombe' Fair had a real religious significance. Whitsun is the Christian festival of Pentecost and the 7th Sunday after Easter. This commemorates the descent of the Holy Spirit on Christ's Disciples. Other places had their own method of commemorating this, including their own fairs.

'Ollacombe' Fair consisted of swing boats, side shows, roundabouts, conjurors, face pulling competitions, sweet stalls and Cornish wrestling. The Billing family were 'top notch' wrestlers at these events. During the 1930s, Annie Mcowen nee Glover fell out of a swing boat and hurt her back. One year in the 1930s whilst the fair was being held in a field at Trewetha Lane, a young David Hoskin was so impressed with the conjuror, that he gave him all his money. The fair was held in various places at Port Isaac including the field behind Trelawney Garage which was called the Pole Field. It then moved to a field behind the Co-op in New Road, and also in the 1930s it used John Hick's field and Doctor George's field which is located as follows: Climb the steps below the Village Hall, and the area to your left was Doctor George's Field. John Hick's field was roughly where Silvershell Road is located.

Joan Dustow said that 'Ollacombe' was a lovely happy occasion for everybody, with wrestling and sweet sellers from Bodmin and Delabole. Marwood Commins resided at Medrose Street Delabole, and he made all his rock, sweets, sweet biscuits

A fair in 'full swing' on the Town Platt. Entertainment came to the heart of the village as when this photo was taken, virtually all of the houses were below a line from St Peter's Church to the top of Rose Hill.
Courtesy of Joe Saundry. C 1900.

This is the only known picture of Marwood Commins. He is seen at the bottom of the picture serving his sweets from his cart at Boscastle Fair. He regularly visited Port Isaac for fairs including Ollacombe Fair and wrestling tournaments.
Courtesy of Brenda Burnard of Delabole.   C 1935.

The reality of social life in Port Isaac for adults and children prior to piped water supplies. The pump in the picture is in Middle Street, which was then named Chapel Street. The lady and girl are unknown.
Courtesy of Arthur Wills.   C1900.

The scene now, with the actual pump preserved. The cottage behind it is now a holiday let in keeping with most of 'old' Port Isaac. Picture by Geoff Provis.   Photo taken in 2013.

and candy floss which he sold at various fairs and events in North Cornwall, including Port Isaac. Other names supplying the sweets etc included Dawe and Hawke.

Ann Steer of Port Isaac also made rock. One year Mr Cummins said to Ann, "I've got ee this year. I've got rock with Port Isaac down the middle."

Ann said, "I'll ave Port Isaac down the centre of my rock by mornin."

The next morning, Ann indeed had rock with the name 'Port Isaac' running through it, and no one knew how she did it, as she could not read or write. Gordon Keat's grandmother possessed the recipe for the rock.

Often these fairs were literally packed with people, as people attended from around the district as well as Port Isaac. Also Port Isaac itself consisted of a high resident population, with cottages actually inhabited by local people.

One factor which assisted the demise of the fairs coming to Port Isaac, was that during one year, two fairs came on the same day, so their takings were down. Apparently things were not the same after that.

The Saturday was sports day, when in olden days donkeys raced up and down the streets. Travelling fairs erected side shows on the Town Platt and in the streets at the bottom of the village. One of the most exciting things for children was to greet the travelling fairs as they slowly came down Trewetha Lane with their large traction engines, and brass work all gleaming. One local resident at the beginning of the century was renowned for winning a wager by entering the lion's cage of a travelling menagerie. He was Jimmy Vickery, and he always emerged from the cage unharmed.

Norman Gregory remembered going to the Fair as a boy when it was held at Short Lane, Port Isaac. He took old rags to give to the fair people, who then allowed him to have a free ride on the swing boats. The rags were used by the fair people to clean the equipment. He said the fair usually came twice a year, once in spring and once in the autumn.   Norman also walked the two miles to St Kew to watch the Cornish wrestling from his cottage on Tresungers Farm.

Village Social Activities.

'Treat' at Port Isaac.

Another very interesting account of a 'Treat' at Port Isaac courtesy of Doctor RJ George appeared in the Royal Cornwall Gazette on the 15th January 1891. No doubt Doctor George carefully selected the date of the event, being the unproductive winter months, so the poor people felt the maximum benefit.

'On Thursday, Doctor RJ George of Port Isaac gave a tea in the Free Church Schoolroom, to about fifty men and women of the place who are in receipt of parochial relief. Tea being over, each received an orange, and a small book as a momento of the occasion. Those that could not attend had a piece of cake and tea sent to them.

In the evening there was a concert and readings to which the public were invited, the proceeds to be devoted to the purchase of coals for the poor of the town'.

This is yet another example of the poverty rife at Port Isaac during this time. The Free Church Schoolroom was the Methodist Sunday School in Roscarrock Hill. At this time the Poor Law was still in existence, and suffice it to say that the poor were in desperate need of help, and charitable giving was an acceptable form of achieving this. I do not deal with the Poor Law in this book, but merely draw attention to persons such as Doctor George, who were very community minded. Thomas Henry Hills, Harry's father each Christmas was given £10 cheques by the 'better off', to deliver to the poor of the village. The Temperance Hall was built in 1895, so other premises were then used for such events.

Talented Locals.

Port Isaac had its share of talented people. An example of this is Robert Mitchell who won a diploma at the West Cornwall Fisheries Exhibition in 1884 for a model of a fishing boat. My late Uncle Raymond Provis, a former fisherman, was an artist, and he also made model boats, sometimes inside a bottle. Making withy pots, and working on their wooden vessels ensured the fishermen were dextrous with their hands.

Port Isaac's First Cinema.

Bessie Selway recalls attending regular film shows commencing during the 1920s at the Temperance Hall. These were held once a week on Thursday nights during the winter by Billy Nute of Delabole. His projector, or contraption as Bessie called it, was placed in the middle of the hall, and Billy turned a handle manually to make it work.

Sometimes the equipment broke down, and the locals stamped their feet, and the children walked around the hall until it re-started. Some of the films were serials which Bessie thought at the time were 'thrilling', and many locals really enjoyed these shows with attendances being excellent. Billy started by showing magic lantern slides before progressing to moving pictures. The local Policeman, PC Cory arranged for his wife and children to enter free to see the shows, and the constable also collected money at the door whilst Billy set up his equipment. If people were late, the PC again at times collected the entrance fees, as Billy Nute was required to work the projector.

Port Isaac's Second Cinema or 'Rivoli'.

The Cinema or 'Rivoli' as it was affectionately known was situated in front of the new coastguard houses, and it was situated at the end of a row of a block which was fronted by the North Cornwall Garage.

This building is the old Port Isaac Cinema, affectionately known then as the Rivoli.
The new coastguard houses are on the right. The Rivoli has been converted to flats.
Picture taken by Geoff Provis. 2013

Up until the Second World War, it was a workshop for the Port Isaac builders, William Taylor & Sons. The War affected the Taylor's business, so Charlie Lobb bought the workshop. He already owned the front end of this row of buildings or sheds, the North Cornwall Garage. Charlie was a big fan of the cinema, and he regularly attended the cinema at Delabole, so he decided to buy Taylors' Workshop, and make it into a cinema.

Initially a concrete floor was put down stage by stage, and Ted Robinson painted murals on the walls of waitresses in evening dresses. Mrs Lobb, Charlie's wife, made the curtains for the front of the cinema which were red with gold braid, and these were always pulled back. Wooden forms were used as seats in the front which were placed on sand, and the seating was arranged according to age, with the youngest nearest the front, and the boys were on one side and girls the other. Railway sleepers were used to hold down the reject cinema seats, which were situated behind the forms. For the later dances, the forms were pulled back. Near the rear, there was a raised area for special seats, which were cordoned off, and had curtains around them.

The 'Rivoli' was opened during the Second World War and Mr Roseveare was the doorman, who was known as 'Rosie'. He was a most unlikely doorman, being very short indeed, and his daughter Lilian collected the entrance fees. Paraffin heaters were used to heat the cinema, plus a round sectioned fire which was lit in the afternoon by Mr Roseveare. On one occasion during the early evening, some local lads climbed onto the roof and blocked the chimney, so the 'Rivoli' became full of smoke.

Charlie Lobb himself initially operated the projector, and all films that arrived had to be re-wound onto another reel. Later Albert Oliver, and Fred Bassett of St.Teath took over operations, and they also undertook similar operations at local places such as St. Breward. The 'Rivoli' found it difficult to get modern films, contrary to the Wadebridge Cinema.

Edgar Bate, a Port Isaac person who was crippled, walked with the aid of a crutch, had a seat especially made for him which was situated half way back on the right as you walked in. Plumes of smoke regularly emitted from Edgar's pipe.

Monday night dances were held at the Rivoli, with live music being provided by the Rivolians, a group led by Mr & Mrs Brimacombe of Port Isaac. Mr Brimacombe, known as 'Brimmy', played piano and xylophone, his wife sang and played the drums, and Hazel Johns Nee Hawken of Blisland, played the accordion. She travelled to Port Isaac by taxi as the dances were very popular, and it was well worth the fare, bringing her to the village. Denzil Flew and his band from Tintagel later played there. Sometimes Ted Grant of the Port Gaverne Hotel played saxophone after closing time, and on occasions a coach full of people arrived from Tintagel to take part in the dance. The Rivolians also played away on occasions.

At the time of the 'Rivolians', concerts were also held in the Temperance Hall, and Ted and Ruth Robinson sometimes performed with Ted on vocals, and Ruth accompanying him on piano. Ruth was a very accomplished artist who used the name Ruth Pinder, and many of her paintings of Port Isaac survive.

A band visited on occasions named The Singers Band. It consisted of Mrs Singer on piano; Anita her daughter on vocals; Jack Thomas of St Minver on accordion; Charlie from Trebetherick, and a female accordion player from St Kew. Jack Provis also played piano on occasions in this band.

A feature I remember well of the Rivoli, was a galvanised shed at one end of the building which gave access to the main door. As youngsters we waited outside the galvanised doors, pushing each other around trying to be the first through the doors when either Charlie Lobb or 'Rosie' opened them. Friday night was the night to see the 'pictures', and once the doors opened, there was a rush to the inner doors which always were shut. There was again an undignified scramble to be the first in, and looking back I feel some sympathy for Charlie Lobb and 'Rosie', both real gentlemen, who had to physically hold us back. Once we got in, we paid 1/3d for the cheap seats, and then sat on hard forms awaiting the usual short trailer such as The Three Stooges.

Harold Spry the coalman had an infectious laugh, and his laughter helped the comedy films no end.

One night a week was devoted to a dance, two nights for the Cinema, and occasionally old time dancing which was danced to a record player.

Lionel Castle occasionally used the Rivoli by arrangement with Charlie Lobb, to show cartoons and entertainment films to the public using his own projector. These were films he hired, and he charged a 9d entrance fee. He also filmed many old scenes at Port Isaac using his own cine camera, and some of these have been transferred to DVD. Lionel died in 1950.

Mrs Brimacombe's Choir.

This choir for girls of between ten and fourteen years, rehearsed at the Temperance Hall, and performed at the Rivoli Cinema during concerts. They formed in about 1949, and at that time I am informed there were no other similar choirs at Port Isaac. Mrs Brimacombe and her husband both had a musical background, and they moved to Port Isaac from another area.

Mrs Brimicombe's Girl's Choir.
Picture taken on the stage of the Rivoli and this is the best quality photo available to me of this group. There was no other choir at Port Isaac at this time, 1948, and they rehearsed and played only at Port Isaac. They performed mainly at the Temperance Hall and also used the Rivoli. Mrs Brimicombe was their tutor.
Back row from the left: Mrs Brimicombe, Eileen Byfield, Jean Glover, Gillian Orchard, Vivienne Donnithorne, Pearl Honey, Diane Mitchell, Janet May, Veronica Keat, Shirley Collings, Doreen Byfield and Colonel Genders.
Middle Row: Barbara Thomas, Jane Galliers, Margaret Hayden, Joy Collins, Gloria Honey, Audrey Collings, Mary Rowe, Maxine Derbyshire, Beryl Byfield, Mr Brimicombe.
Front row: Betty Chadband, Anne Julian, Georgina Williams, Jeanette Honey, Christine Glover, Elizabeth Hayden, June Mitchell, Roberta Derbyshire, Merle Honey. Picture taken in the 'Rivoli'.
Courtesy of Janet Chadband nee May and Merle Arnold nee Honey. C 1948.

A typical old carnival scene at Port Isaac in about 1956. The author Geoff Provis is sitting nearest the lobster pot and his younger brother Graham is at the back on the right.
Provis family picture.   C1956.

The Town Platt.

During the Second World War, on occasions a van parked on the Town Platt and a screen at the rear of the van showed a film for the local youths. Mrs Susie Sherratt, the local baker, also took skipping ropes and spinning tops onto the Town Platt and encouraged the local children to play with them.

During herring fishing, boys hid in the empty wooden barrels stored on the Platt during the hours of darkness.

Singing at Sea.

Tom Brown recalled that on calm evenings along the cliff road, it was possible to hear the Port Isaac men singing whilst their herring nets were drifting in the water just off the coast. A very interesting memory, and one which shows the love of music and singing inherent at Port Isaac.

A very old photo showing a humorous float at Port Isaac Carnival. I believe it was taken in a field which is now Port Isaac Car Park overlooking the bay. The house is the old Vicarage which has recently been converted into a larger building.
Courtesy of Stephen Found.   C 1920.

Carnival Day.

Carnival day was always a great day in Port Isaac and there was always a good entry of decorated carts and wagons, as well as many walking characters. The lifeboat crew often walked in procession wearing their red bobble hats.

Various organisations arranged the carnivals, including the Port Isaac Toc H and even the Wesleyan Chapel Youth Club.

Harmonica Quartet.

I have been informed that the following were members of the harmonica quartet, but I have been unable to confirm this: Harold Spry, the coalman, Tom Collings, a fisherman, Charlie Couch, a mariner and Horatio Clemo of Trelights. These operated in the early 1930s, and they played at local events. Harold Spry was also a member of the Chorale Society, and the Methodist and Wesleyan Choirs at Port Isaac.

Another old picture showing a Prouts' lorry adorned with balloons etc for the carnival.
Courtesy of Stephen Found.   C 1950.

A number of locals enjoy themselves on their float during coronation year 1953. These plucky competitor won first prize.
From the left rear: Shirley Crockford, Pauline Sloggett, Margaret Honey and Bertie Byfield with mask.
From the left front: Les Mitchell,
Margaret Smith who taught at Port Isaac School, Alan Chadband and Ray Glover.
Courtesy of Janet Chadband nee May   1953..

My Uncle Harold Provis served in Italy during the Second World War, and he was impressed by what he saw there. This float was dreamt up by Harold and he called it, 'Come back to Sorrento'. It was entered in the Wadebridge Carnival and members of the Methodist Youth Club participated.
Rear row from the left: Terry ?, and Leonard Crockford.
Middle row from the left: Allison Short, Edith Parsons nee Sweet, Nina Oliver nee Steer, Norren Honey nee Brown, John Tinney Keat and Barbara Honey.
Front from the left: Brian Orchard, Thelma Stone and Dorothy Oliver nee Lobb.
Courtesy of Carol Brogan-Taylor nee Provis.   C1949.

A comical float stating on the placard on the left, 'we can't play the 12th street rag'. On the right it says,
'but we can play the Middle Street ashes'.
Rear row from the left: Nick Bunt and Leonard Crockford.
Second row from rear from the left: John Tinney Keat, Shirley Crockford and Maurice Brown.
Third row from rear from the left: Jean Sweet, Thelma Stone, Noreen Honey nee Brown and John Scott.
Front row from left: Margaret Tucker nee Honey, Ian Honey and Pauline Sloggett.
Standing to the right of the vehicle is Morley Found.
Courtesy of Carol Brogan-Taylor nee Provis.   C 1949.

A super photo of Janet Chadband nee May when she was a carnival queen in 1952.
On the left is Georgina Hocking, and on the right is Barbara Thomas.
Courtesy of Janet Chadband nee May.   C 1952

A very old Port Isaac carnival. Violet Richards informed me that the driver of the leading coach is George Richards, known as 'Georgie Jess' Richards, the father of Jack Richards. Unfortunately I am unable to identify the location.
Courtesy of Violet Richards.   C 1900.

I experienced difficulty choosing which photos of carnival queens to use in my book. However, when I saw this picture I just had to include it, as Georgina Williams was a lovely girl who died much too early.
From the left: Attendants are Mary Mellor nee Hicks, Georgina Williams the Carnival queen and Marilyn Parsons on her right.
C 1957.

St John Ambulance Brigade.

June McCullam nee Lobb, now residing in New Zealand recalls that in about 1953 Doctor Barron's wife asked her if she would start a local branch. Initially it met in the Toc H Rooms which was located just above the Tre-Pol-Pen Hotel, and this building is now named the Smiling Sardine. Doctor Baird of Port Isaac conducted the training lectures based on the First Aid Manual, and June, who had experience of bandaging techniques, assisted the group to pass their exams. There were no uniforms initially, but these came later. June with her husband Francis, and daughter Christine, emigrated to New Zealand in 1955 where June joined the Christchurch Ambulance Brigade.

In 1955, a combined cadet division was formed with Cyril Kinnings in charge, and he informed me that a few dances and concerts were held to raise money to buy uniforms for the cadets. The adult Division consisted of ten members who met on Friday nights for 1st aid lessons. Every year, local doctors conducted examinations in order that the members could obtain a 1st aid qualification. I was a Cadet myself, and enjoyed the experience. On the 1st September 1969, the cadet division amalgamated with the adult division to form a quadrilateral division.

In the early 1960s, the brigade's home was the Odd Fellows Hall at the Wesleyan Chapel, and also the Wesley Chapel School Room. It met during Friday evenings. It was the only uniformed organisation in the village at that time, and was very popular, being led by Mrs Muriel Short and Mrs Kinnings. Obviously, First Aid was taught, but many members studied to obtain the highest award possible which was the Grand Prior badge. In order to obtain this, members studied and passed varied subjects such as home nursing, food handling, child care, fire-fighting, knowledge of the Order of St John, cookery and nutrition, clerical ability, physical recreation, map reading, home craft, road and home safety and interpreter-ship. Each year there was an annual service where St John members from all over Cornwall met up, and it was in a different place each year. By pure chance, the year the service was held at Port Isaac, four local girls won their Grand Prior badge and the service was held at Port Isaac. It took place in Port Isaac car park, and Barbara Hooper was chosen to

A picture of the Port Isaac St John Ambulance Brigade, including cadets, senior members and some prominent village people. Some members were absent, including the author of this book who was a cadet, and the same age as those in the front row.

Back row: Jan Cowling, Anthony Angel, Graham Taylor, Raymond Bate, Trevor Platt, Tony Collins, Dennis Knight.
Third row from front: Mrs Nellie Blake nee Hicks, Mrs Betty Steer, Mrs Doris Mills, Vivienne Donnithorne, Janet May, Christine Bate, Mrs Carter, Mrs Porteus, Mary Rowe, Beryl Byfield, Mrs Muriel Short, Mrs Lilian Kinnings.
Second row from front: Jennifer Martin, Bill Beare, Mr Porteus, Mr Hillman, Cyril Kinnings, Sir Rowland Gerram, (County Commissioner), Clifford Pender, Wesley Blake, Jennifer Porteus.
Front row: Alan Short, Eric Donnithorne, David Sherratt, David Bate, Gordon Hutz, Douglas Mills.
Courtesy of Janet Chadband nee May.   C 1956.

June Lobb who commenced the Port Isaac St John Ambulance Brigade at the request of Mrs Barron, the doctor's wife..
Courtesy of June McCullam nee Lobb.   C1955.

Janet Chadband nee May, and Pat Tucker in their St John uniforms whilst on duty at Polzeath Beach in front of the St John Ambulance hut. C 1956.
Courtesy of Janet Chadband nee May.

Members of the Port Isaac St John Ambulance parade on the beach
having walked around the streets. From the left; Mrs Kinnings, Mary Rowe in uniform, Ray Bate,
and Tony Collins at the rear.
Courtesy of Stephen Found. C 1953.

Five very proud Port Isaac girls display their St. John Ambulance Brigade Grand Prior Badges with Port
Isaac Bay as a backdrop.
From the left: Linda Honey nee Sherratt; Janet Mewton nee Sherratt; Barbara Mckeown nee Hooper; Kay
Bluett nee Rowe and Margaret Kingdon nee Rowe. (Note, Margaret gained her badge previously, and this
is displayed on her sleeve).
Janet is currently a nurse at Port Isaac Surgery, so she has made very good use of her St John training.
Courtesy of Grace Hooper and Barbara McKeown nee Hooper. C 1962.

read the lesson. Following the religious part of the service, four Port Isaac girls were presented with their badges.

Cyril Kinnings proudly told me, that one lady member later qualified as a district nurse, others became a doctor and a captain in the Merchant Service. The local Policeman, Maurice Bearne was a member. During the summer season, they performed duties at Polzeath Beach which included dealing with cut feet, sickness and lost children. It appears from St John Ambulance records that the brigade ceased on 1st May 1975, but I have not been able to verify this.

I contacted Cornwall St John Ambulance HQ & Training Centre at Par for information, and on the 20th August 2008 they kindly wrote to me with the following information:

'The separate Ambulance and Nursing Divisions were formed in 1941. The BFIA and BFIN forms show the following:

Mr CH Scoon OBE DMC TD, Ambulance Divisional Superintendent.

Mrs F Pilborough – Nursing Division Superintendent.

The two Divisions were made into a combined Division in 1951. Mr Billings became the Divisional Superintendent, and Mrs Billings the Divisional Officer.

In 1955 a combined Cadet Division was formed with Mr Kinnings in charge.

The Cadet Division amalgamated with the Adult Division on 1st September 1969 to form a Quadrilateral Division.

The County records show that the Division met at Wesley Chapel School Room, Port Isaac.

The Quadrilateral Divisions were closed on 1st May 1975.

The County records do show Port Isaac Division working with St Minver Division.

The County records also show Charles Symons of Brendon as Divisional President from 1970 to 1973'.   End of quote.

I have been unable to verify or enlarge on the above information from the St John Ambulance.

Shopping Trips.

Although there were a good variety of shops in Port Isaac, during the 1920s, groups of ladies organized shopping trips to Delabole using a Prouts' Carriage. These groups were about four or five in number, and their usual objective was to buy clothes at the Delabole Co-op which then sold a good variety of merchandise. The ladies took the afternoon off for these trips. A young Alf Hooper enjoyed these visits, as he regularly visited Port Isaac with a horse and wagon delivering orders. On other occasions, four or five fishermen's wives hired the carriage for the same purpose if there had been a good catch of fish.

Collecting Sea Birds' Eggs.

Sea birds' eggs were collected, and gulls' eggs regularly eaten as they provided good nutrition, and made a lovely sponge. Once a year my Grandfather Anthony Provis used his boat the *Mapleleaf*, to take a group to Mouls Island near the Rumps if the weather was fine. He put a few of us ashore in a dinghy which he towed there, and we collected easily several buckets of sea birds' eggs of various kinds. This would be much frowned upon today, but at the time the birds were plentiful, and it provided us with some sport and food as a bonus. I now disagree with such practices, but values change with the passing years, so people today should not be too critical of such customs.

Bird Nesting.

Another activity justifiably frowned upon today, was collecting wild birds eggs, and indeed it is against the law. Birds were very plentiful due to the sympathetic environment, and boys took a great delight in accumulating large collections of their eggs. I was very keen on this, and walked many miles; a favourite route being Trewetha, Poltreworgey, Gravlins Lane and St.Kew. To get to Gravlins Lane, turn right at the cross roads above Poltreworgey, and then turn first left. Port Isaac and Port Gaverne Valleys were also favourite spots. Although it was bad for the birds, we were out in the fresh air, and we gained quite a good knowledge of birds in the process. Road traffic was then very light, and as the only entertainment at home was the wireless, healthy outdoor activities were the order of the day. Needless to say, I do not agree with this practice today, but I do wish children would spend more time in the open air.

Cruelty to Seagulls.

A letter to the local press on the 21st September 1895 makes very interesting reading. It shows the value local fishermen placed on the gulls, and confirms that they would not tolerate visitors harming or shooting them. The writer describes the reception such people would receive as 'extremely unfriendly'. This is very interesting bearing in mind the above articles regarding the collecting of their eggs. 'Sir, 				Cruelty to Gulls.

Some of your correspondents have named the Cornish Coast as one of the places where this detestable practice prevails. Let me claim exemption for that part of North Cornwall in which I have been spending my summer holiday. In Port Isaac Bay, gulls are perfectly safe. Their protection may possibly be due to some superstition, though one would hope it arises from simple humanity, but it is the fact that no boatman will take a gun carrying tourist out with him, and any sportsman who is seen gull shooting from the cliffs, will be likely to have an extremely unfriendly reception on his return to the town'.

I include this item to show that Port Isaac was a very hard place indeed during the olden days, and summary justice would have been meted out on those mentioned above.

Port Isaac Womens' Institute.

Formed in 1924, the Womens' Institute met in the Temperance Hall. In 1956/57 it boasted 86 members, but this figure gradually declined with the village changing its character with the increasing sale of cottages for holiday homes etc. The activities of the WI were many and varied, and these played an important role in the social life of Port Isaac. It boasted its own choir and drama group as well as the following activities: an annual outing to places such as Torquay and Paignton; Christmas party, painting, handicraft and cookery classes; flower show, film shows, bring and buy sales, children's parties, whist drives, old tyme dancing and a member's day consisting of games and competitions. These community activities show what a positive effect the institute had on Port Isaac's social life.

Unfortunately membership continued to dwindle, and on the 8th February 1996 it applied for suspension, and the President Mrs Sybil Brown wrote as follows:

'It is with great reluctance and sorrow that the members of the Port Isaac Institute wish to apply to county office for suspension. Port Isaac Institute was formed in 1924, and in November 1994 we celebrated our 70th anniversary. We were honoured with the presence of our founder member Mrs Gladys Bray, but sadly she died some weeks ago. The last two years saw us struggling uphill as our membership dwindled, and those remaining just did not want to stand for office'.

The Port Isaac Women's Institute dressed for an event probably held at the Temperance Hall or Church Rooms. Back Row from the left: Sylvia Julian nee Couch; Marjorie Slatter, Mrs Lewonski, unknown, Nellie Blake, Marjorie Donnithorne, Mrs Oxford, unknown and Sybil Brown.
Front from the left: Unknown, Eileen Prout and Blanche 'Bubbles' Wherry nee Field.
Courtesy of Bill Steer Jnr.   C1950.

Band Nights.

These were a regular feature when I was a youngster growing up at Port Isaac in the 50s and 60s. Bodmin Brass Band visited on Tuesday nights, and St Breward Silver Band on Thursday evenings. The St Breward Band continued to play until recently, but the events during the period I described, and into the 70s and even 80s were really 'local events', when many living in the village, including the lower older portion, attended the concert on the Platt, and they also supported the flora dance played through the streets after the concert. I recall dancing the flora in groups of four, some tuition being given at Port Isaac Junior School. Many visitors asked if they could join in, and they were told to do one, two, three hop, whereas the locals proudly knew the other steps.

A typical scene on the Town Platt as the band entertains the locals and visitors before playing the Flora Dance up the streets. Photo taken from Roscarrock Hill.
Courtesy of Grace Hooper and Barbara McKeown nee Hooper.   C 1980.

After the concert, the band gathered in Fore Street, adjacent the Platt, and the first beats of the big bass drum signaled the start of the flora dance. Slowly the band marched through Fore Street until they reached the school, when they ceased playing before walking up Front Hill. They re-commenced playing just past the Church Rooms, and marched out onto The Terrace playing all the way. On fine summer nights, the repetitive tune reverberated around the village – a real Cornish experience, supported by the then local Cornish population, enthusiastically viewed by the hundreds of visitors. Even the local resident Policeman ensured he was on duty to cover the evening. Regular supporters such as Mrs Dora Glover and Mrs Orchard and Mrs Chadband, stood near the Town Platt in their regular spots to support the evening and have a good natter. When it was over, they, together with their many local friends, disappeared up Middle Street, Fore Street and Church Hill to their cottages, which now have mostly been sold and put to different uses; history indeed!

The band on their return trip, again had the same break, before playing the final session of the flora dance down Fore Street, ending with a hymn at the end, usually 'The Day Thou Gavest Lord is Ended'. Invariably, eager band members adjourned to the Golden Lion for that 'thirst quenching' pint of beer.

Fishermens' Choir.

During the late 1920s, the Port Isaac Breakwaters were being constructed. Following completion of the Eastern Breakwater, building funds were depleted so some men formed a small choir, and they visited surrounding villages to sing and raise funds for the breakwater project. Men in the choir included Altair Bunt, Jack and Tom Collings, Harold Spry and Sam Honey.

A super photo showing the excitement generated by the flora dance at Port Isaac many years ago. The band has stopped outside of the school while the children continue to dance around. I recall taking part in this during my younger days, and I confirm that locals of all ages showed a great interest in this regular event.
Courtesy of Stephen Found.   C   1955.

Bodmin Town Band leading the flora dance past the Church Rooms.
Courtesy of Grace Hooper and Barbara McKeown nee Hooper.   C 1980.

Bodmin Town Band leading the flora dance past the Church Rooms.
Courtesy of Grace Hooper and Barbara McKeown nee Hooper.   C 1980.

Port Isaac Male Quartet.

I have been informed that the following were members of the Port Isaac Male Quartet, but I have been unable to confirm this: Harold Spry, John Prout, Horatio Clemo of Trelights and Tom Collings. These operated in the 1930s.

Temperance Hall.

Built by, and for the Band of Hope in 1895, this hall has over the years been used by numerous village societies for events too numerous to mention, and you will note mention of it in many sections of this book. Many plays and variety concerts were enacted there, including of course meetings of the Band of Hope which is discussed in the section on chapels. The WI regularly staged plays there, and Pat Smythe and Mrs Jack Hicks, two local teachers did likewise. During the 1960s in the summer months, weekly plays were performed by the local amateur dramatics group, and Alf Hooper and George Bartholomew were leading members. I recall seeing Alf perform his monologues as Jan Stewar, and he was very talented indeed.

The hall has played an important part in the social life of the village, being used by numerous organisations, sports clubs and for entertainment. Two dances a week were held in the hall, and these were known as the 'Sixpenny Hop', as of course the entrance fee was 6d. On occasions Jack Provis, played the piano. Merle Arnold nee Honey recalls walking to dances at the old St Endellion Church Hall and St Kew Hall during the 1950s. She said that boys walked from St Mabyn, St Breward and Delabole to attend the dances, and that sometimes the boys walked the girls to Port Isaac before walking back on their return journeys.

Numerous talented locals over the years have performed there. One of these was a Bessie Billing, a spinster, who told yarns about real local people at concerts and visitor's concerts, using the Cornish dialect. She also owned a parrot.

In the summer of 1951, the Port Isaac Drama Group performed 'Sit Down a Minute, Adrian', by Jevan Brandon – Thomas, a comedy in three acts. The cast was as follows:

Ed Fletcher..............George Bartholomew.
Joan   ....Shirley Crockford.
Adrian Sparkes ....John 'Brigadier' Reed.
Dorothy   ....Maud Grant, a professional actress.
Florence Hedley ....Mini Prout.
Nicholas................. Tommy Atkins.
Bertha.................... Lilian Genders.
Marcia.................... Margaret Smith, a local school mistress.
Joe Gorm.................Maurice Brown.
Betty.................... Mavis Pam.
Abel Johnson............ Gordon Dovey.

It was produced by Pat Porteous. Tickets were sold by Mrs Cowling of the Drug Store, Mrs Lansdowne of the Lucky Piskey Gift Shop and Miss Thelma Stone. Lighting was by Mr Angel, and carpentry by 'Brigadier' Reed and George Bartholomew. The play was performed on every Tuesday thoughout the summer of 1951.

The Delabole Optimis Company visited thc hall on occasions, and they presented a variety show. Mr Nute, a Blacksmith of Delabole did a monologue, and their comedian was named 'Boxer' Rowe. Part of his act was to conduct, and as he did so his arms grew longer. It is believed that if 'Boxer' was alive today, he would be quite famous.

Concerts were held at the Temperance Hall before the National Health Service, to help pay for the village nurse, who before the Second World War actually lived in Port Isaac. John Neil helped by walking around Port Isaac collecting 2d a week from families; one penny for the Nursing Association and one penny for thc Ambulance. The only Hospital was in Bodmin.

Plays were performed there by local drama groups, and choirs practiced and sang there.

At one stage, only ladies toilets were available in the hall, and the men went outside to relieve themselves against the walls. Mrs May Brown and Mrs Theresa Lobb held whist drives to raise money to pay for mens' toilets to be built; another example of community work.

I recall dancing around the maypole in the hall, and I include photographs of this. Prior to 1895 when the hall was built, maypole dancing was conducted in an old disused quarry in New Road Port Isaac, which was almost opposite the Co-op. In the 1880s, grass covered the quarry, so it was indeed very ancient. The quarry was finally filled in when New Road was laid.

The Delabole Optimis entertainment group which played at the Temperance Hall on several occasions.
Back row from the left: Wilfred Hawke, Edwin Williams, Irvin Thomas.
Front row from the left: Leonard Cowling, 'Boxer' Rowe and Jack Moore
Courtesy of Brenda Burnard.   C 1935.

From the left: Mary Hills Billing, wife of Pascoe Billing; Elizabeth Jane Billing, wife of Dick Rowe; and Bessie Billing, spinster. Bessie owned a parrot, and on occasions appeared in concerts at the Temperance Hall, telling stories with a Cornish accent and imitating local characters.
Courtesy of Mary John.   C 1895.

The full cast of Port Isaac Drama Group on 3rd April 1951, taken at the Temperance Hall during the play, 'Sit Down a Minute, Adrian'.
Names of the cast, although not necessarily in order are as follows: George Bartholemew, Margaret Smith, Gordon Dovey, Mavis Pam, Tommy Atkins, Shirley Crockford; Mini Prout, Maurice Brown; Mrs Genders, Maud Grant and Brigadier Reed.   (Details of the Play are in the text).
Courtesy of Redruth Cornish Studies Library.   1951.

The cast of the pantomime Robin Hood played at the Temperance Hall Port Isaac in about 1950. Mrs Brimacombe played the piano, Elsie Richards directed and Ted Robinson assisted. At this time Port Isaac School also produced pantomimes organized by the Headmaster Boss Richards and his wife Elsie.
The two back rows from left to right: Merle Arnold nee Honey, Velma Knight nee Collings; Mrs Evans, Edith Parsons nee Sweet; Ruth Robinson, Eileen Byfield, Shirley Gladwin nee Collings - 'Robin Hood'; Jill Orchard, Doreen Byfield, James Platt, Ann Thomas, Jean Glover, Christine Glover, Ted Robinson and Mrs Brimacombe.
Front row: Joyce Hambly nee Masters; Margaret Honey, Ann Irons nee Julian; Jean Spry, Audrey Collings, Tony Robinson, Trevor Evans and unknown.
The 'panto' played for several nights to good crowds.
Courtesy of Merle Arnold nee Honey.   C 1950.

I have seen a few references to an annual Port Isaac Flower Show, but I have been unable to find any details or anyone with a memory of it. One gentleman said it was held in the Temperance Hall, and that during the early days many wild flowers appeared in it, but he could not enlarge on that sparse information. It was apparently an important event in the annual calendar of events at Port Isaac.

Auctions.

Very often if a house was to be sold in the village following a death, the contents were sold by auction at the Temperance Hall. These auctions were well attended as many people at Port Isaac were very poor. A professional auctioneer usually came from Wadebridge to conduct affairs. Sometimes the hall was quite full of furniture and people, with the side door being some distance away from the main entrance. This occasionally led to some quite comic situations, as people could not always tell who was at the other end of the hall. Joe Saundry continues the story:

'One morning mother said the spout of the bellows had come off so she couldn't blow the fire.

A concert scene taken from 'Sailor Beware' performed at the Temperance Hall on Tuesday nights throughout the summer in about 1959. During the peak six weeks the hall was packed. Brigadier Reed and George Bartholomew were the 'driving forces' behind the productions.
From the left: Merle Arnold nee Honey, Brigadier Reed who also produced the play; and Nellie Blake nee Hicks.
Courtesy of Merle Arnold nee Honey.

George Bartholomew on the left and Alf Hooper dressed as a Policeman whilst performing a play for Delabole Amateur Dramatics. Both were heavily involved in Port Isaac plays at the Temperance Hall, and indeed, both lived at Port Isaac.
Courtesy of Grace Hooper and Barbara McKeown nee Hooper.   C   1960.

A Christmas play at the Temperance Hall organized by Port Isaac School.
From the left: Unknown, Jean Williams – kneeling; Mary Mellor nee Hicks; unknown and Nora Keat.
Courtesy of June McCullam nee Lobb.   1953.

A scene from the play Sailor Beware performed at the Temperance Hall.
The three ladies in front from the left: Ann Irons nee Julian; Mini Prout and Pat Rowe.
At the rear from the left: Charles Griggs,
possibly George Bartholomew, Merle Arnold nee Honey and Brigadier Reed.
Courtesy of Merle Arnold nee Honey.

Father said, "Tis auction sale up the hall today – probably they'll have one. I can't go, I've gotta go Port Gaverne to see me cows."

Anyway he came back in time, and went in the side door of the hall.

Mother said, "I don't suppose he'll be back, I'd better go up."

Mother went in the main door. The bellows came up for auction, father one end bidding, and mother at the other end bidding.

Eventually the bellows were knocked down to father, and when he got home he said to mother, "I managed to get the bellows."

Mother didn't let on that she was also bidding and 'running up' the price. When they tried the bellows, they discovered it had no valve in it'.

Joe said that he furnished his first house for only £14 in such a way, as he could not afford new.

Yarning.

'Yarning' was literally the 'talk' of the village, and it defined the character of Port Isaac. There was a distinctive Port Isaac accent, totally different from Tintagel and Delabole, and also different from Wadebridge and Padstow. I recall signing for Delabole Football Club at the age of fifteen, and I was amazed at the new Cornish accents I was hearing. Previously at Wadebridge School, I was able to immediately identify a Padstow accent. A school mate of mine, Rodney Constance always pronounced the word 'fishing' differently to us. He always accentuated the 'ing' in 'fishing', as did other Padstow children. This loss of identity and individual traits is a high price to pay for this perceived age of progress.

Fishermen enjoyed talking to each other about old times, the weather, good catches, ship wrecks or anything associated with the sea and not least of all, tell funny stories about present day or old characters. Contrary to what people may think, there was little bad language used by the men. They did of course swear, but it was mainly the 'b' words, never what I would term really bad language. Fish cellars were an obvious place to meet, especially where lobster pots were being made. There always seemed to be many older retired fishermen around for a chat. This also made the time go quicker for the men making the pots, as that was a very repetitive job. There was a slight risk with the withy pot, as if anyone got too close, the 'bindage' could whip around and catch you in the face. I have seen this happen, and I can assure you there was no sympathy from the people present.

During inclement weather, the men met in the passage way beneath the Market House on the Platt. This provided shelter from the wind and rain. There were a number of meeting places, and most had a view of the harbour so the men could view the harbour activity. Locally these meetings were called a 'Parliament'.

Tobacco was very short or unobtainable during the war years, so local men often made up a concoction of herbs to smoke, which by all accounts smelled horrible. Surprisingly one common ingredient of this was the yellow petals of the ragwort plant.

A superb photo showing the local Maypole dancers. Local people including parents and family members of the children sit at the front and back of the Temperance Hall watching the children. Traditionally people danced around tree poles in celebration of the end of winter and the start of fine weather to allow planting to begin. This occurred in Cornwall as well as the rest of England. The gentleman standing nearest the camera on the left is Harold Spry who was involved in a wide variety of entertainment at Port Isaac. The gentleman standing on the right is Mr Hillman who similarly was involved with many social activities. The boy standing in the centre of the front is John Welch. The lady standing on the right is May Brown, the wife of Tom Brown. May taught children the flora dance, and was also involved with other social events.
Courtesy of June McCullam nee Lobb.   C 1951.

Maypole dancers singing in the Temperance Hall. It is difficult to place each person and some are unknown. However, the following is a list of some present: Eileen Bunt, Christine and Jean Glover; Doreen and Beryl Byfield; Ginette Honey, Ann Julian, Molly Hook, Nora Keat, Ruth Robinson, and Jean Williams.
Courtesy of June McCullam nee Lobb.   1951.

May Day celebrations at Port Isaac during the early 1930s. The May Queen, Olive May Welch nee Mortimore born in 1923 is seen in the centre wearing her crown. From then on Olive was referred to as 'Queenie'. Courtesy of John Welch.   Early 1930s.

A photo from early in the twentieth century of an unknown event at Port Isaac. The gentleman in the centre of the back is William Glanville Mutton, known as 'Dan', my great uncle; and the front right is Norman 'Ningy' Short. Courtesy of Stephen Found.   C 1925.

Three elderly Port Isaac ladies having a 'yarn' in front of the Slipway Hotel. Another photo displaying the vast change brought about in Port Isaac.
From the left: Louie Lobb who married Captain Frank Lobb, Beatrice Provis nee Lobb who married John Provis the great-grandfather of the author and Liza Oaten nee Lobb. (Lizzie Miller nee Lobb, a sister of Beatrice and Liza, and the mother to Bernard Miller was not in the photo).
Provis family photo.   August 1935.

Circus.

Pre War, the circus came to Port Isaac, and was located at the bottom of Mayfield Road where the new school is situated.

I recall in the 1950s attending a circus in the field above Garrick Trewetha lane, which is now the childrens' play field.

Also on occasions the circus set up in Hick's field, which is where Silvershell Road is located.

The circus visiting Port Isaac located in Hick's field opposite the council houses. The photo was taken from 6, The Villas, Trewetha Lane by Harold Provis. Note the prefab in the background. Courtesy of Carol Brogan-Taylor nee Provis. C 1950.

Bird Beating.

Bird beating consisted of a few men walking off into the countryside with a lantern and armed with sticks. The lantern consisted of a box with a candle in it and a glass front. The object was to shine the light into the eyes of roosting birds, and knock them down with the sticks, and any breed of bird was targeted. Favourites were starlings and song thrushes, which were known locally as 'grey birds'. The best time was in bad weather with a strong wind, as the birds were easier to catch under those conditions. Birdie pie was made by skinning the birds, cleaning them and putting them in a pie. Again this was a means of obtaining cheap food, but sport was the main thing which interested the men. John Lark, a cobbler, Jack Provis and Dick Rowe, both mariners and fishermen regularly went bird beating together. Bird beating was practised for hundreds of years.

Another way of obtaining birds for consumption was when the herring nets were being dried after being barked. Sammy Keat owned the Bark House in Dolphin Street, and also some land at Short Lane. This is the first lane on the right going out of Port Isaac past Hillson's Close, and the field used for this purpose was the on the left at the end of the lane. The nets were placed on the fields to dry, and at night when the birds settled down in the fields they were caught in the nets. The local youths went to Short Lane in the mornings to collect the dead birds. The main catch with this method was song thrushes.

The reader studying these words today may be horrified at such practices, but general hardship, lack of money and work, allied to no welfare state, meant that the men folk had to obtain their food and protein from sources available naturally.

Rabbiting.

Killing rabbits for sport and food was an important past time carried on by local people over much of the country, and not just Port Isaac. The rabbits provided good low fat nourishing food which was high in protein, and was much appreciated by the residents. Many men over the years have caught rabbits, and special rabbit nets were made at the Port Isaac school by the pupils, such was the importance of the cheap nourishing rabbit in times of need. Gin traps, which are now illegal, were set in the rabbit runs, and dogs were used as well.

Rabbiting was not without its dangers. In 1918, Bill Spry Snr, a seaman who then lived at Plain Street, was out rabbiting when he failed to secure the trigger on his shotgun. A twig or branch caught in the trigger, and the shotgun severely injured one of his legs.

Port Isaac Brownies.

Grace Hooper formed the Brownies in about 1975, so she was the 'Brown Owl', and was helped by Barbara Richards and Judy Vague. Twice Grace took the Brownies to London, and they were allowed inside the gates of Buckingham Palace to see the Changing of the Guards which had been pre-planned. Grace was always full of energy, and some of the youngsters had difficulty keeping up with her. Grace continued as 'Brown Owl' after the normal retirement age, as no one was available to take over from her. When Grace finally stopped her Brownie duties, they found it difficult to replace her, so they eventually ceased sometime in the mid-eighties. However, Cindy Powell and Melanie Dingle nee Wherry continued with the Brownies, and again later Jennie Tiddy carried the work on, but I do not deal in detail with their work in this book. They all agree that it was a very useful organization to teach the girls discipline and working as a team. There are no Brownies at Port Isaac at present.

The now defunct Port Isaac Brownies pictured near Rock. The adult supervisors in the background from the left are Judy Vague, Grace Hooper, the Brown Owl and Barbara Richards nee Finnemore.
Children from the left: Sarah Gifford, Julie Bishop, Ellen Philp, Justine Rowe, Tanya Richards, Heather Collins, unknown, Irene Roberts, Ellen Gaunt, unknown, Mandy Shay, Antoinetta Dawe, Donna Hambly and Belinda Burman.
Courtesy of Grace Hooper and Barbara Hooper nee Mckeown. C 1980.

Surfing at Polzeath.

During the 1950s and 1960s, when transport was more available, a favourite past time was surfing at Polzeath, being only six miles away. Flat wooden surfboards were used, and of course there were no wetsuits. Swimming at Port Isaac and Port Gaverne was also popular, but the thrill associated with the Polzeath surf was, and still is something special.

Visitors' Concerts.

An interesting series of visitor concerts took place at Port Isaac over many years, which strongly suggests there was much affection for visitors. I also know of cases where visitors have formed 'life-long' friendships with local people. The first of these concerts was reported in the Royal Cornwall Gazette on the 31st August 1899:

'In aid of the funds of the Port Isaac branch of the RNLI, a concert was given on Friday by lady and gentlemen visitors, and as Port Isaac has this season an unusually large number, an admirable combination of musical talent was secured. Encores were frequent, and the visitors gave a large share of patronage'.

During the 1930s, annual visitor concerts were held in the Church Rooms, and Lionel Castle performed a ventriloquist act with a dummy named Joey, and he was very good. The income from bed and breakfast or letting apartments was important to 'old' Port Isaac, and the visitors fell in love with the old village, and made numerous friends with local people. The balance then between locals and visitors was sensible, and the two co-existed amicably.

Visitors pose for a photo at a holiday let overlooking the harbour at Port Isaac. They have just dressed for a visitor's concert, 'The Tower', a mime at the Temperance Hall. (This photo was found in a small album of photos in West Cornwall and I have no idea as to the identities of the participants).   C   1948.

Members of the now defunct Port Isaac Historical Society dressed in period costume. For a period they did excellent work recalling Port Isaac history, collecting old photos, finding and copying the Trevan document and bringing this to the attention of the public.
Ladies from the left: Rita Strickland standing alone on the left; Liz Rowe, ?, Gwen Hambly, Yvonne Cleave nee Leverton;, Noreen Honey nee Brown; Janet Chadband nee May, Elaine Found nee Short and Christine Saundry.
Men from the left: Peter Rowe, Ian Honey and Ledville Cleave.
Courtesy of Janet Chadband nee May.   C 1995.

Joey Honey pictured on Port Gaverne with three young 'visitor' girls. Local characters made friends with visitors, and this was hugely appreciated by the visitors themselves. Regular holiday makers have told me they regret the changing nature of the village, and that they miss the character of the old village.
Courtesy of Joan Murray nee Honey.   C 1930.

Jack Collings – 'Pyscador a Gan' - Fisherman of Song.

Jacks' career as a bass/baritone soloist took off when Dr Wilson Gunn, who was the conductor of Wadebridge Male Voice Choir heard him sing at St Kew School Room in 1925, and from that time on encouraged and developed his career. At music festivals in 1927 he won thirteen first and three silver medals. He was also known as the 'Fisherman Bass'.

His first broadcast on the radio was in 1928, and was transmitted from the Foster Hall, Bodmin. It was so well received that he secured a contract with the Decca Record Company and he made several '78' rpm records, travelling to London with his pianist, Christine Hoskin of Port Isaac. One dealer, Napier and Sons of Wadebridge, sold five hundred records of Jack's sea songs in the first week. His repertoire, understandably, was mainly about Cornwall and the sea. He broadcast

Jack Collings, the 'well known' Port Isaac singer.
Courtesy of Peggy Philp nee Collings. C 1940.

regularly from 1928 onwards, and was a first choice to sing at the annual Devon and Cornwall Festival at Central Hall Westminster.

During the War and just after, he enjoyed singing with the Delabole Optimis, a small concert party who entertained widely. Jack was for much of his career accompanied on the piano by Mrs Clemo of Trelights.

Jack continued to broadcast regularly for many years, and in 1946 sang again with St Dennis Silver Band at the Foster Hall, Bodmin. Shortly after Jack suffered a fractured skull after falling from a ladder and thereafter lost his will to perform, since he was convinced that he was not achieving the same quality. Even now his records are occasionally heard, and 'Summercourt Fair' was broadcast from Radio Cornwall a couple of years ago. There is no doubt he had a very fine voice, and his interpretation was superb.

On the night of the 23rd January 1939, the 'Medea' was lost on Greenaway Rocks, Trebetherick Point, the St Ives Lifeboat was lost with the loss of all but one crew, and the Padstow Lifeboat was temporarily lost in the terrible weather. See my previous book, 'The Seafarers of Port Isaac'.

On the 26th February, at 8.15 pm, a special concert was held at the Palace Theatre Bodmin in aid of the St Ives lifeboat Disaster Fund. The chairman was Captain Atkinson, coxswain of the Padstow Lifeboat 'Princess Mary', supported by the

Mayor of Bodmin Mr ST Hoare, Esq. The soloist was Mr Jack Collings of Port Isaac, who sang 'Sea Fever' by request in the first half, and a selected song in the second. Jack was accompanied by Sydney Hearn. Also appearing were the Bodmin Town Band, and Bodmin Male Voice Choir. The programme closed with the hymn, 'Abide with me'. Admission by programme was sixpence.

Jack and his two brothers were fine singers. It is significant that he always said that his brother Tom had a better voice, but he refused to sing solo. His younger brother Leonard also had a good voice, and together they could represent a good bass line in any choir.

Jack was initiated a Cornish Bard in 1946, taking the Bardic Name

Jack Collings appeared also with the Delabole Optimis group.
Jack is second from the right at the rear.
Courtesy of Terry Gifford.   *C 1935.*

'Pyscador a Gan' – 'Fisherman of Song'.
Richard and Sarah Parsons of Port Isaac.

For details of the musical achievements of the above couple, please see the section on Port Isaac Chapels dealing with the Methodist Chapel.

Port Isaac Chorale Society.

Sometime after World War One, Harold Drabble of Homer Park formed the Port Isaac Choral Society, he having moved to Port Isaac from London. It came into being in the early 1930s from the annual Bible Society Meeting which was held at the Temperance Hall.

Mr James, the manager of L Chapman & Sons, Green grocers of Fore Street, Port Isaac was the choir master, and he was responsible for the society. They were a mixed choir who met and rehearsed at the Church Rooms. They sang a mixture of harmony and madrigals, and Muriel Couch accompanied on piano. A notable member was Tom Collings, the brother of Jack, who had a rich deep bass voice.

Port Isaac Chorale Society taken at Bide-a-While Hotel, Port Gaverne.
Rear row from the left: Harold Spry, John Prout, Jack Thomas, Mark Prout, Tom Collings, Sam Honey, Mr Wearne,
Mr Nankivell and Mr May.
Standing just in front of rear row on the left is Mr Drabble, and on the right is John Tucker.
Second row from back from the left: Eileen Prout, Inez Cory, Mollie Williams, Bessie Selway, Mrs H Spry, Mrs Hicks,
Cassie Saundry, Mrs Nankivell, Joyce Honey, Betty Creighton and Nancy Bunt.
Front row from the left: Olive Williams, Barbara Honey, Mrs Cory, Muriel Couch, conductor Mr James; Mrs Ashton,
Mrs England, Mrs Kendall, Gladys Collings and Muriel Tucker.
Courtesy of Stephen Found.   C 1930.

Tom could not read music so he practiced privately with Muriel Tucker. The photo
was taken outside the Bide-a-While Hotel, Port Gaverne, the owner of which was
Mrs Ashton, the deputy conductor of the society.

The society broadcast from Bristol, Bodmin Foster Hall and at Camelford where
they mixed with another choir to broadcast hymns. Soloists were sometimes brought
in from outside, and they entered various competitions. The shield in the picture was
won at such competition. The usual complement of the society was 31.

In March 1936, the society, conducted by Ronald James, with Catherine Wendoll
– Soprano, and Alexander Henderson, bass, broadcast from the Temperance Hall on
the BBC Home Service. Until recently a couple of small cup shaped objects were
visible near the main doors which were associated with this broadcast.

Before the Second World War, Mr James moved to Bristol, and someone from
Bodmin took over, but the society did not survive very long after these changes.
Prouts' coaches were used for all their transport.

Harold M Drabble (1878-1957), Founder of the Chorale Society.

Harold was born on 1st September 1878 in Sheffield, the youngest and the
eleventh child of Rev Peter Drabble. He became an engineering apprentice on the
Clyde when ship building was at its height. At the outbreak of the First World War
and at the age of 36, he was called up and saw services in the trenches in France and
Belgium, and also at
Gallipoli. He married Lalla Bull, and had their first child in 1913.

After the War, he moved to London and the Home Counties, before settling at Homer Park, Port Isaac, finally retiring to Wadebridge.

Howard M Drabble, (1878-1957), who formed the first Port Isaac Chorale Society. See text. Courtesy of Richard Hoskin.

The 'Present' Port Isaac Chorale.

The modern Chorale began about fifteen years ago as a result of some men in the village wanting to sing with some confidence in the pub! Also, Janet Townsend felt that after 23 years of directing the highly successful Port Isaac Singers she needed a change of repertoire. They then met with some of the ladies choir for a good sing in the Village Hall, previously the Temperance Hall, under the leadership of Janet Townsend. The men ultimately became the Fishermen's Friends, while several of them, mostly with their wives became the Chorale, and sang in it for many years. The choir has continued to grow in number, with members from around the area. Relatively few concerts are given, but the aim is enjoyment, and leaving practices on Tuesday nights having had a good sing and feeling better for it.

The modern Port Isaac Chorale was formed by Janet Townsend about twelve years ago. Full details in text. This picture was taken at the Bide-a-While Hotel, Port Gaverne, as the Chorale won the same trophy as the older Chorale, so the members thought it a good idea to pose in the same place.
Tenors: Peter Rowe, John Lethbridge, Brian Richards, Nigel Sherratt and Liz Rowe.
Basses: Ernest Tucker, David Ward, Jon Cleave, Michael Mabley, George Oxley and George Steer.
Sopranos: Sarah Kinsbury, Dee Randell, Caroline Cleave, Sue Flitter, Elaine Found, June Bryant, Rosemary Williams, Anne Steer, Margaret Tucker nee Honey, Jo Sherratt, Esther Dudley, Barbara Oxley and Sue ?
Altos: Carol Lee, Kathy Carney, Carol Hurd, Barbara Richards, and Linda Ward.
Accompanist: Maureen Wakeham, Musical Director: Janet Townsend.
Courtesy of Janet Townsend.   C 2001.

They boast a wide repertoire, and over the years have raised several thousand pounds for charity.

The Port Isaac Singers.

The Port Isaac Singers first sang together in 1970. They were formed initially by Janet Townsend MBE as a choir to sing carols in the Wesley Chapel. Originally a mixed choir, as so few men came forward, they became a very successful ladies choir.

During the next twenty three years, they competed in music festivals all over the West Country, Blackpool and Cheltenham where they even won the Gold Cup – not the horse race, but the overall choir trophy for all classes of choirs. At the Cornwall Music Festival, they were the first to be awarded the Edgar Kessell Trophy which is awarded to the overall choir performance.

Television appearances included 'Opportunity Knocks', when Hughie Green was presented with a pasty, and twice in the televised performances of Sainsbury's Choir of the Year competitions where they represented the South West. They also took part in the Inter-Celtic Festival in Brittany for Cornwall, performing 15 concerts in 10 days and having a very memorable time in the process. The 'fun side' was the many concerts all over Cornwall, always followed by magnificent Cornish suppers, but above all the friendship and support the members had for each other over the years.

The Port Isaac Singers pictured in the Wesley Chapel at Port Isaac with the small Bugle Festival cup, and the Wadebridge Music Festival cup.
Back row from the left: Joan Murray nee Honey, Merle Arnold nee Honey, Ann Irons nee Julian, Joyce Hambly nee Masters, Ida Brown, Pauline Stephens nee Brown, Yvonne Cleave nee Leverton, Christine Saundry and Jean Batten.
Front row from the left: Clarinda Truscott nee Blake, Josephine Provis nee Boehm, Sylvia Kemp, Shirley Gladwin nee Collings, Elaine Found nee Short, Joan Orchard, Avis Wills, Velma Knight, nee Collings, Christine Hawkey nee Beare and Barbara Richards nee Finnemore.
Janet Townsend, musical director, and Joan Grainger, accompanist.
Courtesy of Merle Arnold nee Honey.   1971/72.

The Cellar Boys.

During the very early 1960s, nearly every small town or village boasted a pop group, and Port Isaac was no exception. You must remember, this was the early days of Rock & Roll, and the shadows were hugely popular. Indeed, it was very exciting times musically, and everything seemed new and fresh. Our group consisted of David Sherratt, lead guitar; Jimmy 'Shan' Langton, drums; Billy Hawkins, guitar; and myself Geoff Provis on guitar. We practiced in John Sherratt's Garage in Trewetha Lane. The highlight of our career was playing at a social function for Delabole football club at the Tintagel Castle Hotel. We also played at the Temperance Hall and at a couple of local villages. Billy recalls that at one stage we wore the same type of trousers.

We obtained our drums from Mrs Carling at the butcher's shop in Church Hill, as she informed us she owned a set with the name 'Rivolians' written on the bass drum, which had been lying in her attic for years. Our amplification was so poor compared to present day gear, that it defies description. My amp was a 'Goldenaire' which consisted of a few valves plugged into a steel chassis, and it was not even in a cabinet. Our music was mainly shadows instrumentals, but looking back now it was all very exciting and new. Were we the first pop group at Port Isaac?

Billy Hawkins eventually moved away from Port Isaac, but he continued his music career by singing and playing guitar in rock and soul bands. He returned to Port Isaac in 1995, and although he had many friends in the folk scene, he turned his attention to songs of the sea, eventually helping form the Fisherman's Friends shanty group.

Port Isaac indeed has a rich musical history, and I do apologise for anyone I have omitted. I recall as a youngster, sitting listening to older men 'yarning' down by the harbour, when on occasions Norman Short produced either a pair of spoons or bones, and proceeded to place them in one hand and play them with some dexterity. I remember thinking at the time how magical this was, given the setting in which Norman performed. Jimmy Baker of Middle Street, many years ago possessed a trombone which on occasions he played in the street. He also played it at the Golden Lion, but on one occasion he knocked several pints of beer off of the bar so was sadly banned. It is however, impossible to cater for everyone in a book of this nature, so I do apologise if I have missed some well deserving person.

Jack Provis was taught to play the piano at the age of 16 years by Gladys Donnithorne of Port Isaac. He wanted to play the organ at the Methodist Chapel at Port Isaac, as it boasted the best sounding instrument, however, although Susie Sherratt said he could do so, 'Jennie' Hills and Mrs Tucker said he could not. He therefore played for St Peter's Church. He continued his musical career playing for other churches including St Kew, and St Endellion; for Mrs Singer's band which regularly played in the Temperance Hall and in a duet with Bob from Bodmin who played the xylophone. During World War Two he played piano for the Coldstream Guards and the NAAFI.
Courtesy of Warwick Provis Snr & Jnr.
C   1950.

Lionel Castle of Atlantic View, Port Isaac, with his ventriloquist dummy named 'Joey'. Lionel also used six marionettes in his act, which he performed in the Church Rooms and Temperance Hall and especially at Visitor Concerts. (The marionettes were also named humanettes, and were about two feet tall and with a large head). Lionel also showed films at the Rivoli, performed at children's parties, and filmed some old scenes of Port Isaac on his cine camera.
Courtesy of Peter Larkin.   C 1935.

Christiana Edmonds Hoskin, (1891 – 1967), was born in Port Isaac on 16th January 1891. Her parents, Richard and Sarah Parsons were both accomplished musicians as well as committed Methodists. Christine, as she became known, learnt the violin from the age of 4, giving her first public performance at the age of 7, and went on to become a talented pianist with a remarkable gift for being able to memorise a complete set of music after hearing it only once. She taught piano, violin and singing. She married Richard Hoskin in 1914, and moved to London, returning to live in Port Isaac in 1948. She continued to teach piano to Port Isaac children, and it was during the 1950s that she started to lose her sight. During this period she composed the majority of her hymn tunes. Her setting of Christina Rossetti's poem 'Love Came Down at Christmas' is her most enduring work, and is still sung at Port Isaac to this day. Christine also accompanied Jack Collings on piano on his 78 rpm records.
Courtesy of Richard Hoskin.

Priscilla Milne, (1928-2007). 'Musycyen Portyssack'- Musician of Port Isaac.
Priscilla Milne nee Hoskin was trained at the Royal Academy of Music and devoted much of her life to teaching music at schools in Shropshire, St Austell and Stover Newton Abbott. Following her marriage, she lived near St Kew, and taught piano to many Port Isaac children. She also founded the Treforest Singers in Wadebridge, which included Michael Collings from the well known musical Port Isaac Collings family. I recall hearing the Treforest Quartet singing at the Temperance Hall and they were excellent. In 1995, she won the Cornwhylen Cross for musical composition at the Cornish Gorsedd with her composition 'Pader Agan Arluth', (The Lord's Prayer in Cornish). In 1996, she won the Gorsedd Bert Thomas Cup for composition 'Fond memories'. In 1997, she was installed as a Cornish Bard as above in recognition of her work for Cornwall.
Courtesy of Richard Hoskin.   1977.

Josephine Provis, nee Boehm, (1927- 1985), the author's mother. Josephine spent her early years at Saltash where she sang regularly at church, Plymouth Notre Dame School Choral Society, and in concerts. Following the Plymouth blitz in 1941, she moved with her family to Port Isaac, this being the ancestral home of her mother, Edith Mutton. She quickly became known for her clear soprano voice, and sang solo many times at the Temperance Hall and other similar establishments. (See picture in community celebrations section on page 61). She married Cyril Provis of Port Isaac in 1946, and she continued to sing at music festivals and with the Port Isaac Singers where she sang solo on occasions. (See picture in Port Isaac Chapel section on page 184). She also sang solo whilst accompanied by Eve Faulkner, Janet Townsend's mother on piano. Famously on occasions, Port Isaac's singing butcher, John Hicks, refused to serve her in his shop, unless she sang either with him or for him.
Provis family picture.   C 1945.

In 2011, Janet Townsend was awarded an MBE 'for
services to music and to the community of Port Isaac'.
As well as forming the Port Isaac Singers and Port Isaac
Chorale, she has been a church organist, school governor,
parish councilor and magistrate for twenty two years. Full
details of the 'singers' and 'chorale' are in this section.
Photo courtesy of Janet Townsend.   2011.

Les Mitchell - 'Myghal Porth Ysak' – Mitchell of Port Isaac.
Les emigrated to New Zealand from Port Gaverne in 1958, and four
years ago he was made a Bard of the Cornish Gorseth for services to
the Cornish in New Zealand. For forty years Les has been secretary of
the Christchurch Branch of the New Zealand Cornish Association. Les,
and his sister Heather are the only surviving founder members of their
branch. Les is pictured wearing his Cornwall jersey which also displays
his Bardic name tag.
Courtesy of Les Mitchell.   C 2010.

David Castle has played piano by ear for very many years
until the present day. Locally he regularly played at pubs and
at concerts in the days when the piano was really appreciated, and was the most popular instrument of entertainment.
He was also the pianist for the Frank Fuge Band based at
Plymouth, and he regularly travelled there to play. He also
played for this band at the Thurlestone Bay Hotel in Devon
whilst holding down a full time job at Port Isaac. Now in his
eighties, he continues to play at hotels whilst residing at Fuer-
taventura. I have heard him play, and he really does play in
an entertaining manner, with his feel and interpretation of
melody being first class.
Courtesy of Pisces and the Rev Peter Larkin.

Janet Chadband nee May pictured at Buckingham Palace having received her MBE from Her Majesty the Queen. This was awarded 'for services to charity and to the community in Port Isaac'. Janet has organized fund raising events such as charity meals, coffee mornings and cake stalls for various charities, including the Home Farm Trust, the mentally handicapped, and the churches and chapels. Also, Janet has cooked food for numerous local events, and has worked hard to ensure the modern Port Isaac retains a vibrant community.
Picture courtesy of Janet Chadband nee May.
3rd December 2002.

Clarinda Truscott nee Blake – Conores
Porthysak – 'Singer of Port Isaac'.
Clarinda is pictured with her husband Keith during the initiation ceremony whilst becoming a Cornish Bard awarded for 'services to Cornish Music'. Her Bardic name being 'Conores Porthysak - 'Singer of Port Isaac'. Keith received a similar award although he is from Indian Queens. Both sing together at numerous events throughout Cornwall, and of course at many chapels. Clarinda commenced singing at Port Isaac Wesley Chapel Sunday school and anniversaries. She is a mezzo soprano, and has also sung solo at music festivals and with the Port Isaac Singers.
Courtesy of Clarinda Truscott nee Blake.   *1st September 2001.*

Heather Gladstone nee Mitchell of New Zealand, formerly of Port Isaac and Port Gaverne. Heather sat next to me at Port Isaac School before emigrating to New Zealand with her family at the age of 10. She received musical tuition at Port Isaac from Christine Hoskin who urged her never to give it up. Heather has received numerous awards for her musical career including NZAA Teachers Certificate, Bachelor of Music University of Canterbury, Bachelor of Music (Hons) Canterbury, Certificate of Merit for outstanding services to accordion; Vernon Griffiths Prize for Musical Leadership Canterbury University, and Music Specialist in Schools SW England. There are numerous other awards which I shall not detail here. She teaches accordion and voice, has visited Cornwall on many occasions and has worked for the County Education Authority and performed at the Royal Cornwall Show. She is passionate about Cornish music, and has taught and performed many Cornish carols in New Zealand. Also she has formed choirs including a choir in St Albans, New Zealand where no auditions are necessary, just a desire to sing, and this is going very strongly indeed.

Courtesy of Heather Gladstone nee Mitchell. Taken at the Canterbury Accordion Association 29th September 2013.

Heather Gladstone nee Mitchell, conducting at the Canterbury Accordion Association, on the 29th September 2013. Courtesy of Heather Gladstone nee Mitchell.

The Fisherman's Friends of Port Isaac, who have won national, and even international fame for their rendition of sea shanties. They have appeared at Glastonbury, and won an award at the BBC Folk Awards for 'Best Traditional'.
From the left: Jon Cleave, John McDonnell, Peter Rowe, Jason Nicholas, Billy Hawkins, John Lethbridge, Trevor Grills, Julian Brown, Jeremy Brown and John Brown.
Courtesy of Trio, Jon Cleave and Billy Hawkins.

Geoff Provis was a member of Port Isaac's first pop group the Cellar Boys, and received the music prize at Wadebridge school for violin playing. Since 1995 he has performed 1,514 gigs at hotels and clubs in Devon and Cornwall as a solo entertainer.

Frederick George Mortimore received the MBE in 1966 in recognition of his political and public services. He was the clerk of the works in 1940/41 to 1945/46, and responsible for ensuring airfields were built by contractors up to a standard needed by large WW2 aircraft, and for liaison with US forces in the area. In 1948 he moved to Teignmouth where he continued his public duties returning regularly to Port Isaac to see his in-laws, Les Keat, Jim Lobb and families. Pictured from the left: Cynthia Lewis nee Mortimore, Olive Mortimore nee Bate, Frederick George Mortimore and Olive Welch nee Mortimore.
Courtesy of John Welch.   *1966.*

Port Isaac Chapels and their Activities.

The chapels were of the utmost importance to Port Isaac, and their influence extended way beyond the religious aspect. Their various services, celebrations, youth clubs, Sunday schools, parades, bazaars, fetes, festivals, Boys' Brigade, Band of Hope, concerts, 'outings', friendly societies and choirs were a vital part of 'old' Port Isaac. Whilst reading the following paragraphs, I ask you to consider the extent of the loss to the village of their demise. Their contribution to the history of Port Isaac is vast, and they helped to set the social fabric and tone of the community from the days of John Wesley. I have been told that in the early days, it was necessary to arrive a half an hour before the 6 pm Sunday service at the Methodist Chapel, in order to have a seat.

Sunday schools were a useful addition to the education available at the time, and provided the opportunity for children to read and write, helped by their willing teachers.

Chapel 'outings' from the days of horse travel were immensely popular, and these afforded the poor population the opportunity to travel and visit places previously inaccessible. Indeed, for some poor families this was the only opportunity for the youngsters to leave Port Isaac for a 'short break', so you may understand why it was considered a 'treat' during the early days, to go to Polzeath for an 'outing'.

Local families living in the country walked many miles to attend their chapel. Norman Gregory, whose family numbered seven, recalled living in a two bedroomed cottage on Tresungers Farm, and walking the three and a half miles to attend Trelill Chapel for harvest festivals.

I do not deal with the interesting history of Methodism in Cornwall, but suffice it to say that the various factions of Methodism re-united in 1932 following the previous splits in the movement. However, in places such as Port Isaac, the Wesleyan and Methodist chapels continued to be named as before, and families kept the same loyalties to their particular chapel. There was a friendly rivalry between the two chapels, although on being re-united, some Wesleyans said they had 'come back home'. The Roscarrock Hill Chapel was the Methodist Chapel, and the chapel in Port Isaac Valley was the Wesleyan.

I discussed in my book, 'The Fishermen of Port Isaac', the value and meaning of 'Sunday' to Port Isaac people in olden days.

Bessie Selway, a Methodist said, "There was Sunday school at 10 am and 2 pm, and services at 11 am and 6 pm. To be in village life you entered into chapel activities, and you were expected to go years ago, and it was the done thing. Mother would not allow us to sow or knit on a Sunday, and she would say, "You've got all week to do that."

My Grandfather Mark Bishop never did anything on a Sunday, and he wasn't religious. You see, Sunday school gave us somewhere to go, and we met our friends." David Hoskin said that on Sundays, swings were taken down at his family home, and the only reading allowed was the Bible and Pilgrim's Progress.

Anita Bunt nee Couch who was born in 1918 said, "All we had was the beach really, the Band of Hope and Sunday school. At the Methodist Chapel the very young ones, about six or seven years old had a separate teacher, Mrs John Hicks, and they met in an anti-room separate from the main Sunday school."

The Methodist Chapel.

The Methodist Church in Roscarrock Hill, previously the United Methodist Free Church, was opened on the 27th June 1869, replacing the old chapel which was originally opened in 1837. The old chapel was then used as a Sunday school. The new chapel is on the right when viewed from Port Isaac Harbour.

A super photo showing the location of the Methodist Chapel in Roscarrock Hill. The chapel is on the right of the Sunday School. The building immediately in front of the chapel is the old Industry pilchard cellar which is still used by the fishing concerns. The chapel was not only physically close to the sea faring industry, but was supported by many seafarers and it meant so much to many of them.
The Winifred lies on the sand at the front of the other boats which have their bad weather covers on.
Rear row of boats from the left: Gleaner, Victor, Boy Terry and Boy Harry. The two in front of them from the left are the Hope and Dawn, and the two in front are the Mapleleaf and Winifred.
Courtesy of Grace Hooper and Barbara Mckeown nee Hooper. C 1960.

'The earliest record of a chapel at Port Isaac is 1770, and a chapel society existed there since the 1750s, the time of John Wesley'. (TS).

Beneath the Sunday School is a large room which was originally used to store coal brought to Port Isaac by the sailing vessel *Telegraph*. Following this, half of it was rented by Sunday school Superintendent John Stone to stable his pony. Harry Hills, the chapel stalwart and local builder and undertaker then used it as a store and as a place to build and repair boats.

At the chapel opening, a public tea was held on the Town Platt. The chapel seating was originally in the region of 400, and for many years it was filled with worshippers on Sunday evenings, and was renowned for its fine congregational singing. The valley side of the gallery was often filled with fishermen in their blue jerseys, and some of their favourite hymns were brought home to the chapel by the fishermen or sailors themselves, who in some distant parts during their travels heard

The interior of the Methodist Chapel in Roscarrock Hill during harvest festival time. Note the ornate paraffin lamps suspended from the ceiling and the general pleasing layout including the withy lobster pots. Note also that later the pulpit was moved. Courtesy of Maurice Brown.   C 1930.

a tune which they liked, and having committed it to memory, brought it home to Port Isaac. Bessie Selway said that the singing during the winter months was marvelous, and that one row of men had a lovely bass sound. She said the service started with a Bible reading, a prayer, and then the community singing followed by the sermon. Usually the men sang on the Town Platt before the 6 pm service, whilst walking up and down in their familiar manner as described in my previous books. The public generally did not like to hear the choir sing, as they wished to join in themselves.

Bessie said that harvest festivals were the same with the harvest hymns, and Christmas time with the carols, some of which were unique to Port Isaac. The Selway family always walked to the chapel from Port Gaverne, whatever the weather.

In the New Year, Bessie visited houses collecting the 'seat rent' of six shillings from individuals requiring a booked seat for the year, and families requiring a whole pew paid £1. 4s. Stalwart chapel members, some of whom rented pews including the following: Warwick Richard Guy, Will Taylor and family; Thomas Henry Hills, Harry Hills and family; Avery family; Blake family of Trewetha; Mr & Mrs Sam Stephens; John Stone and family, Sherratt family, R Broad, Susan Couch, T Mitchell and J Hawke.

Few places of Worship are as close to the sea as this chapel, and it was surely a very moving experience to be present during such splendid singing from a large congregation in the light and warmth of ornate paraffin lamps. On occasions, the wind was 'howling' outside, with rain beating on the windows, and one wonders how many times the iron window frames have been replaced over the years due to the salt spray.

The interior taken from the same position during normal times. Note the pine panelled ceiling. Also some of the gallery is visible where much superb congregational singing occurred.
Courtesy of Maurice Brown. C 1940.

Christmas 1967, three chapel stalwarts meet at the Roscarrock Methodist Chapel.
From the left: Susie Sherratt known as 'Gran' Sherratt, Alf Hooper and Bessie Jane 'Jennie' Hills. All three gave a lifetime of devotion to chapels.
Courtesy of Grace Hooper and Barbara McKeown nee Hooper.

Doreen de Mott was evacuated to 25 Chapel Street, Port Isaac during the Second World War. She said, "I enjoyed going to the chapel in Roscarrock Hill, sitting upstairs and hearing the wonderful voices of the fishermen singing so well, and dressed in their dark blue fishermens' jumpers. It made going to chapel a pleasure, and was inspiring."

One tradition was that the fishermen always remained seated for the second hymn, whereas usually all congregations stand for all the hymns, but I do not know the origins of this. However, from April to October, the fishermens' seats remained largely empty, as the men were away serving as crews on the yachts of the Peerage.

When the new chapel was opened, the choir sat on a circular seat beneath the rostrum, and prior to the installation of the pipe organ, they were accompanied by a harmonium played by Mrs Sarah Parsons, and her husband Richard Parsons on the violin.

The pipe organ was installed in 1917 at the back of the chapel replacing the harmonium, and the choir then had their seats in the gallery by the organ. The organist was Mrs G M Tucker who played for many years whilst Tommy and John Sherratt busily pumped it.

Harvest festival was the first Sunday in October, when all the oil lamps were lit which made the chapel quite hot. It was also well decorated with apples around the gallery, and lobster pots, nets and various produce adorned the chapel with vegetables in the windows. All this produce was sold at 7 pm on the following Monday night after the service and tea, and the proceeds sent to hospitals. The harvest festival services were all well attended at 11 am and 6 pm on the Sunday, and at the Monday evening service, with Anglican people also in attendance. People wore their Sunday best, and the ladies wore hats. The Wesleyans celebrated their own harvest festival.

Over the years the folk were called to worship by a bell recovered from the wreck of the *Bencoolan,* a sailing vessel wrecked near Bude. The bell hung on the roof of the Sunday School Hall, and its history was inscribed inside the chapel. Briefly, the *Bencoolan* was wrecked near Bude on the 21st October 1862, and there are two stories as to how the bell reached Port Isaac. The official version is that it was purchased by Thomas Hills, the grandfather of Harry Hills for 30/-, and brought to Port Isaac in the smack *Telegraph* of which he was master. However, Frank Rowe Jnr, a very astute man and a relative of the Hills family, informed me that the bell was brought to Port Isaac by the Hills family in a pony and trap. I merely relate both versions to you.

There is also inside the chapel, a memorial for those from the village who died on service during the First World War. The old notice board outside the chapel was made by Mr TH Hills, (Harry), a local carpenter, undertaker, boat builder and chapel stalwart. He purchased the wood used for this in 1904, when he had the task of repairing the fish cellars opposite, which had been damaged by heavy seas.

Dorothy Tucker on the left, and her sister Bertha Blake; both Port Isaac Methodist stalwarts for many years. Dorothy was a Methodist Missionary, and gave many years service abroad. Bertha was an organist at the chapel for many years.
Courtesy of Grace Hooper and Barbara McKeown nee Hooper.   C

In the days of the watch-night service, the large congregation came from the chapel to sing on the Town Platt, their voices rising across the water in the first hours of the New Year.

Features of the chapel were good sermons and favourite hymns and tunes, two examples of these being, 'There is a green hill far away', and at Christmas, 'Hark the glad sound the Saviour comes'. My Great-Grandfather John Provis often said, "That was a 'bitiful, bitiful' sermon."

The original lime ceiling was replaced by the very nice wood panelled ceiling by Harry Hills, and David Cowling of Pendoggett. Numerous people have been prominent members of the chapel over the years, including in previous years William Mitchell until 1895, Captain Tom Mitchell, Tom Collings, and Miss Bessie Jane 'Jennie' Hills who gave a life-time of service in the choir and Sunday school. During winter evenings, with gales, driving rain and sea spray against the windows inside the chapel, the light and heat was coming from paraffin lamps, carefully primed and tended for many years by Mrs Hancock, the caretaker. She resided, with a friend, Jack Williams, in a small bungalow built by John Neal below Wara Tara Quarry, Church Hill. This was the very last house near the top of Church Hill, and recently a far larger building replaced it. Other Methodist stalwarts included Mrs Mary Phillips, Susie Sherratt, the Hicks family and Maurice Brown.

Poster Proclaiming the Opening of the New Chapel in 1869.
'United Methodist Free Church.
PORT ISAAC.

The members of the above church have pleasure in announcing the following services in connection with the opening of their new chapel on Sunday June 27th 1869. Three services will be conducted as follows:

In the morning at 11 o'clock, a sermon will be preached by Mr WJ Harley of Rochdale.

In the afternoon at 2.30 pm an address will be given to the Sunday school scholars, teachers and parents by Mr John Ashworth of Rochdale, author of 'Strange Tales of Humble Life', who will also preach in the evening at 6 o'clock.

On the following Tuesday, June 29th, Mr Ashworth will preach at 11 am. A luncheon will be provided at 1 o'clock.

During the afternoon a bazaar will be opened with a good assortment of useful and ornamental articles.

A public tea will be provided at 5 pm, and in the evening, Mr Ashworth will deliver a lecture subject, 'Young Women, Wives and Mothers'. Chair to be taken at 7 o'clock.

On Wednesday June 30th, Mr Ashworth will again lecture, the subject "Young Men, Husbands and Fathers." Chair to be taken at 2.30 pm. A public tea will be provided at 5 pm. In the evening a public meeting will be held to be addressed by Messers Ashworth, Harley, the circuit Ministers and others. Chair to be taken at 7 pm. During the interval of services, the bazaar will be re-opened.

On Sunday July 4th, two sermons will be preached by Mr J Jenkin of St Columb. Service in the morning at 11 o'clock and in the evening at 6 o'clock. Collections will be made at the close of each service in aid of the building fund.

No charge of admission to the lectures.

Tickets for the luncheon and teas one shilling each, and admission to bazaar 3d.

R Wakefield Printer and Bookbinder Fore Street Camelford'.

I understand the tea and luncheon were held on the Town Platt, and the Sunday School used for the bazaar.

Band of Hope.

The Port Isaac Band of Hope was established in 1870, and so enthusiastic were its members that they built the Temperance Hall in Trewetha Lane in 1895, now the Village Hall, and they held their annual festival there. Band of Hope members had to abstain from alcoholic drinks, tobacco, opium and study the Bible. Members believed that alcoholic drinks were fatal to the health and happiness, peace and prosperity of their family and community. Many members signed a 'pledge' promising to abide by those rules. However, at Port Isaac, following a row sometime before 1920, the Band of Hope split into two groups; the Wesleyans joined with the Church of England to form one, and the Methodists the other.

The Wesleyan and Church of England Band of Hope were nicknamed the 'Corklegs', after Miss Corkhill who taught piano, sewing and painting after school time. They were also referred to as the Temperance Band of Hope, no doubt because they met in the Temperance Hall. Their feast days and parades were led by Camelford Silver Band, and they led the procession through the back lanes and hills, and across the beach. Anita Bunt nee Couch remembers in her young days marching through the village holding the string streamers supporting the banners up Front Hill,

An early photo of the Port Isaac Band of Hope taken on the beach, with the Pentus in the background. The gentleman on the right proudly displaying his Band of Hope medal is Mr Corkhill, a local coastguard, chapel and Band of Hope stalwart   *Courtesy of Stephen Found.   C1900.*

along The Terrace and down Back Hill. At that time there were very few houses in New Road, so the parade did not venture there. Two men carried the flag, and four women held the streamers to keep the flag steady. An interesting point is that Anita attended the Methodist Chapel with her maternal Grandfather John Stone, but her family were members of the Wesleyan Band of Hope, such was the interesting split of loyalties. Initially, the Methodists held their Band of Hope Day on Wednesdays, and the Wesleyans or Temperance Band of Hope held theirs on Saturdays, but eventually The Methodists also moved to Saturday.

Following the strenuous exercise of carrying banners and flags, and garlands of flowers, free tea was provided for the children consisting of splits and saffron cake followed by a public tea. The adults paid for their tea which included fruit cake. I wonder if there are many people left who in a moment of nostalgia on entering the Temperance Hall remember the aroma of freshly baked bread, saffron cake and various other cakes. Prominent members included Willie Symons, Letitia Corkhill, Mr Corkhill, Mrs E Brown, Guy Hawken, Wesley Blake, Harold Provis, Charles Symons and Harold Spry. Many years ago there was fierce rivalry between the two

Band of Hope medal given to Harold Provis by Miss Corkhill. The medal was presented to 'stalwart members' of the Band of Hope. This is now in possession of the author.
Photo by Geoff Provis.

Band of Hope organisations, and an example of this is as follows: One day during the early days of the twentieth century, Henry Tom was riding his horse 'Lady' down Church Hill, and was riding past the quarry when he saw two men fighting, and he noticed that blood was flowing freely. He tied 'Lady' to a tree, and took the men by the scruffs of their necks and parted them, and asked what they were doing. He knew them both, and one was a member of the Wesleyan Chapel at Port Isaac, and the other a member of the United Methodist Chapel, and they were fighting over which chapel had the best Band of Hope. Henry managed to reconcile them, and they later became good friends.

The original second new Band of Hope flag, purchased sometime between 1910 and 1920 to lead the annual procession. Cost - £100. This flag has been renovated by Annie Philp and helpers. Photo by Harold Provis.   *C1950*

The 'Timberlegs', the Methodist Band of Hope, used the Methodist Sunday School for their meetings, and held their own separate parades. Before a parade commenced, baskets were decorated with flowers, and they were judged first, second and third; and these were then carried in the procession. Initially they marched up Rose Hill on the cobbles, and then around the village including The Terrace, but later they ceased using the Rose Hill route as it was too arduous. They did not venture onto the beach, and no uniforms were worn. The band, usually the St Minver band, led playing marching type music, and large banners were carried by the men with the ladies holding the streamers. The parades usually started between 2 pm and 2.30 pm.

The original Band of Hope flag dating from 1870. Annie Philp of Port Isaac found this flag and its counterpart rotting beneath the stage of the Temperance Hall, so with the help of Sue Rescorla of St Columb and a small band of volunteers she renovated both flags which are now on display in the above hall, now the Village Hall. Well done girls!   Photo by Harold Provis.   C 1950.

After the march, tea was served in the Sunday School, (see details later). After tea, everyone adjourned to the sports field for an afternoon of sports. Entertainment for the children included such activities as racing, putting oranges under water and letting the children put their faces beneath the water to search out and claim

St Breward Silver Band leading the Band of Hope procession in New Road by Hick's corner. The local Police Constable is Maurice Bearne. The young man standing in the gateway is James Platt. The girl holding the flag rope in front is Gloria Honey, and the lady at the rear is Kath Thomas. The man on the right holding the flag is Cyril Provis, the father of the author.   *Provis family photo.*   *1955 or 1956.*

The Wesleyan Band of Hope girls during a parade, marching on Port Isaac beach. Note the fisherman, Tommy Tabb relaxing on his boat the Ben-My-Cree in the background, and people watching the proceedings from Little Hill.   *Provis family picture.*   *C 1954.*

one. Treats with treacle on them were hung up, and the children tried to eat them without using their hands thereby getting treacle on their faces. First of all, sports day was held in Doctor George's field, and then it moved to the field above Garrick in Trewetha Lane which is now the children's play field. Doctor George's Field was located as follows: At the top of the steps below the Temperance Hall there are some bungalows immediately on the left, and these are located on what was originally Doctor George's field. Prominent members were Tom Collings, Jack Hale Thomas, Bill Cowling, Mr & Mrs John Lovell Brown and Mrs Tucker. The flora dance was performed after the parades, led by the St Minver Band.

The Band of Hope day was one day a year, normally in June or July. One interesting fact is that the pubs always sold more beer on Band of Hope Day, probably as a rebuff to the views of those taking part. Mr Irons, the licensee of the Golden Lion in the 1930s always purchased more beer leading up to Band of Hope Day. The picture denotes the parade outside of Hick's Butchers Shop, and my father Cyril is the one on the right holding the banner.

The two separate Band of Hope organisations were quite opposed to each other, and it was common for one to wish 'bad weather' on the other for their respective parade days.

It may be easy today to pour scorn on those people with such strident anti-alcohol views, but in those days when poverty was so common, any money earned was needed for the family. There were of course a few examples of known drinkers spending their wages very quickly on alcohol, and leaving their wives and families with no money for the forthcoming week, and in the days before Social Security and the Welfare State, that was a very serious matter.

Baskets of flowers having just been judged in the children's competition during the Band of Hope Day. Following judging, these were carried around the village during the parade by the children.
Provis family picture.   C 1955.

Delabole Silver Band during a break on the beach during a Band of Hope Parade.
Provis family picture. C 1954.

Port Isaac Band of Hope in procession by the Pentus in Fore Street. In front from the left: Miss Lakeman and Mrs Sweet. The lady behind on the left is Alice Brown.
Courtesy of Harold Provis.   *C1953.*

Band of Hope members commencing to proceed through Port Isaac in a revival of the festival during the 1950s. Note, they have just walked out of Short lane, which is the lane above Hillson Close, Trewetha Lane. The two men carrying the banner are Harold Provis on the left, and Harold Spry. The two ladies on the ropes on the left are Alice Brown on the left and Miss Lakeman. The lady on the right looking away from the camera is Dora Glover, the wife of John.
Provis family photo.   C 1953.

Band of Hope 'Outing' to Fowey.

The local Band of Hope also organised outings for their members, and on one occasion the Band of Hope visited Fowey. A special attraction at the harbour was to be rowed out around two racing yachts for 6d each, so several of the members availed themselves of this opportunity. However, it soon became apparent that one of the men rowing the youngsters was drunk, as he nearly fell overboard. Monica Welch was appalled that a drunken man was rowing a small boat which contained her daughter. The drunken man said that if any of them could row they could. Stella Honey took the oars, and rowed the punt out and around the racing yachts Endeavour and Shamrock. An unexpected bonus was that a few Port Isaac men were crewing on these yachts.

Report of Christmas Festivities, Royal Cornwall Gazette 31st December 1896.

'Port Isaac United Band of Hope Christmas Festivities were held in the Board School on Boxing Day, and consisted of a Christmas tree, a public tea, and an evening's entertainment. The Christmas tree was gaily decorated with useful and fancy articles which met with a ready sale. The tea as usual was well patronised, and the refreshment stall attracted considerable attention. The evening's entertainment consisted of tableaux vivants, musical drills, and vocal and instrumental music'.

Band of Hope and Blue Ribbon Army Meeting – Methodist Sunday School.

A very interesting report in the Royal Cornwall Gazette of 11th May 1883, gives fascinating details of a meeting at Port Isaac which included the Padstow Volunteer Band.

'Friday was the last day selected for the holding of the Blue Ribbon Army, and the Band of Hope, and a most successful affair ensued, the Padstow Volunteer Band being in attendance at the headquarters, viz, the Methodist Free Church Schoolroom.

I apologise for the poor quality of this photo, but I wanted a photo of these Wesleyan and Band of Hope stalwarts, and this is the only one I have. Photo taken at the entrance to the Temperance Hall.
From the left: Letitia Corkhill, Willie Symons, a very influential Wesleyan and Band of Hope member and Mrs E Brown.
Courtesy of Harold Provis.   C 1925.

In the afternoon a procession was formed, headed by the band, and marched to the room where an excellent tea was provided. In the evening, a crowded meeting was held, the chair being taken by Mr Mark Guy, and excellent addresses were delivered by the Rev EF Tonkin and Messrs A Hawkey and J George. The choir ably rendered several songs, under the conductor Mr Hammett, and Miss Horden presiding at the harmonium. Perhaps the most amazing portion of the entertainment was provided by Mr James Furse, who gave several performances on the concertina, creating a deal of laughter by his mimicry. The meeting was one of the most successful ever held here, between sixty and seventy persons taking the Blue Ribbon'.

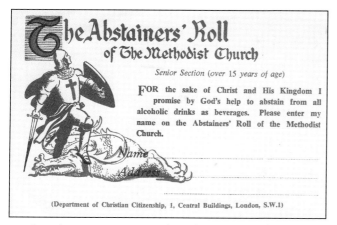

Another report states that the ten members of the band had a narrow escape whilst returning to Padstow. They boarded a rowing boat at Rock, and during the crossing they noticed a foot of water in the vessel. Some wanted to swim for Padstow, but the bandmaster persuaded them to stay with the boat and row as hard as possible. On landing, the boat was almost full of water and on the point of sinking.

Note:

The Blue Ribbon movement was founded by Francis Murphy, an American. The society promoted 'anti-alcohol' ideals of temperance, and encouraged people to find pleasure and enjoyment in other Christian activities. The above report explains in graphic detail the enthusiasm locals exhibited for the Band of Hope. Port Isaac history indeed, but an important part of the developing character of the village. The locals, many of whom were poor, were prepared to publically display their loyalty to this 'anti-alcohol' movement, knowing that many in the village disagreed with them.

The following details are taken from three posters relating to the Port Isaac Band of Hope , and I hope they give you a feel of the public involvement and organization involved.

The Wesleyan Band of Hope girls on parade carrying their flower baskets, closely watched by Wesley Blake, the Wesleyan stalwart. From the left: Ann Philp, Jennifer Smith nee Parsons, Jennifer Martin, unknown and Clarinda Truscott nee Blake. Courtesy of Stephen Found.   C 1954.

PORT ISAAC UNITED BAND OF HOPE.

The Annual Festival will be held on Wednesday, July 5th, 1939. The Procession will leave the Temperance Hall at 2.30 pm accompanied by the Delabole Prize Band. Floral Exhibits, both Garden and Wild Flowers, including a class for children over 5 and under 7 years, must be at the Hall not later than 1 - 30 o'clock.

Artistic Designs will count greatly with the judges. Exhibits must be carried in the procession or prizes will be forfeited.

Free Tea for the Children at 4 o'clock.

Public Tea at 5 pm., price 1s.

Public Meeting. At 6.45 pm at which the lady judge will distribute the prizes for Floral Exhibits, and the band will play suitable Selections.

Collection for the Sports which will immediately follow.

A Dance will be held in the hall from 9 – 30 pm till 1 am. Admission 1/3.

Torquay Accordion Dance Band.

Quintrell & Co., Printers and Stationers, Wadebridge.

The following details taken from a poster advertising the choosing of the Temperance Queen, plus the Band of Hope Festival Day in 1955.

Festival Day, Saturday, 23rd July, 1955.

3 pm, Crowning of the Temperance Queen in the Church Room. The Floral Exhibits will also be on view. Admission 6d.

Floral Classes, Floral Designs and Decorated Baskets.

Garden Flowers: Class 1 - Age 4 to 7 years, Class 2 - 8 to 11 years and Class 3 - 11 to 14 years.

Wild Flowers: Class 1 - 4 to 7 years; Class 2 - 4 to 7 years; Class 2 - 8 to 11 years; Class 3 - 11 to 14 years.

Prizes in each Class: 1st - 5/-; 2nd - 3/-; 3rd - 2/-. Consolation Prizes to all Entries.

All Exhibits to be in the Church Room by 1.30 pm for Judging and all Exhibits to be Carried in the Procession.

4.15 pm. Tea in the Temperance Hall for all Band of Hope Children.

All children of the Parish up to the age of 14 years inclusive, who wish to enroll as members, collect TEA TICKETS at Wesley Hall, on Tuesday, 28th June at 6 pm.

5 pm. Public Tea in the Temperance Hall. Price 1/6.

The Band will be Playing Outside the Temperance Hall from 3.30 pm onwards.

6 pm. The Procession will leave the Temperance Hall, headed by the Queen and Attendants and St Breward Silver Band.

7 p. Public Meeting in the Temperance Hall. The Band will play Selections and the Childrens' prizes will be presented. A collection will be taken.

8 pm Childrens' Sports to be followed by the Flora Dance.

ELECTION OF THE TEMPERANCE QUEEN AND ATTENDANTS.

The Election will take place on Thursday, 7th July at 8 pm in the Temperance Hall.

Supporting Concert by Local Artistes and Visitor Talent. Spotting Competition.
Admission 2/- and Voting Paper. Children half Price. Entry ages, Queen - 9 to 14,
Attendants 4 to 9.
Entries to be handed to the Secretary by Wednesday 9ᵗʰ June.
H Provis, 6 Council Houses, Hon. Sec.

The following details taken from a Band of Hope Festival poster in 1956.

PORT ISAAC BAND OF HOPE FESTIVAL
Saturday, 7ᵗʰ July 1956.
Floral Exhibits to be taken to the Temperance Hall for judging by 1.30 pm.
Floral Designs and Decorated Baskets:
Garden Flowers: Class 1 - Age 4 to 7 years; Class 2, 8 to 12 years.
Wild Flowers: Class 1 - Age 4 to 7 years; Class 2, 8 to 12 years.
Prizes in each class: First 5/-, Second 3/-, Third 2/-.
Consolation prizes for all Entries.
The Exhibits will be on View from 2 pm. Admission 3d.
All Exhibits to be carried in the Procession.
4.15 pm, Tea for all Band of Hope Children up to 14 years inclusive.
Public Tea in the Temperance Hall at 5 pm, Price 1/6.
6pmthe Procession will leave the Temperance Hall, headed by the Carnival Queen
and Attendants and St Breward Silver Band.
7.15 pm, Childrens' Sports, followed by the Flora Dance.
8 pm Film Show. Children Free: Adults : Collection.

Richard Parsons, a staunch Methodist and leading member of the Port Isaac Methodist Chapel until his move away.
Courtesy of Richard Hoskin.   C 1910.

Richard Parsons, 1864 – 1944; Sarah Parsons nee Bennett 1870 – 1930.

I make no apology for including the above married couple, even though Richard was originally from St Teath, and Sarah from Padstow. Richard was a cobbler and violin teacher at Port Isaac, and Sarah a Port Isaac School Mistress. Richard's cobbler's workshop was behind the Golden Lion, where he made boots and shoes for the villagers, and also the gentry. I have not been able to discover the exact location of this shop, but a possibility is that it is above the steps which are visible at the bottom of the 'ope' next to the pub.

They lived with their children, Christiana, Bertram, Frederick and Bennett at 'Tredethlin', Front Hill, Port Isaac, now named 'Trethoway'. Both Richard and Sarah were God-fearing parents, but strict disciplinarians with alcohol, tobacco and playing cards, tools of the devil, being banned from the home. In keeping with other Port Isaac people including the fishermen, Sunday was their day of rest, the Sabbath being observed totally, with no work being done, and the children attending Roscarrock Hill Chapel four times for services and Sunday school. They were however different to most Port Isaac families, they being rather aloof and relatively well off financially. They also exhibited very strict values on many matters.

Sarah Parsons, the wife of Richard, and an important figure musically in the history of the Methodist Chapel. Courtesy of Richard Hoskin. C 1910.

However, on one occasion when Richard was poorly, a neighbour said to Sarah, "How's Richard now?"

Sarah said, "It's Mister Parsons to you, and he's none the better for your asking."

Even Richard and Sarah's family felt in awe of them. They were 'Godly people', and 'holier than thou', and they never apparently put a foot wrong.

No doubt, the majority of their friends were among the Methodist congregation, where their efforts for the chapel were greatly appreciated.

Port Isaac breakwaters were completed in the late 1920s, so when the children were young during the very early days of the century, the seas regularly swept up over the Town Platt during high spring tides, which then had not been cemented over, and the waves crossed the road. This happened sometimes when Richard and his family were walking to chapel in Roscarrock Hill, and Richard would shout, "Stand back and wait."

When the waves retreated he shouted, "Run."

They all then ran to Roscarrock Hill and safety.

Often Richard played his violin at chapel, accompanied by his wife Sarah on the organ. During bad weather if there were rain and gales, Sarah turned up the volume of the organ, and the fishermen increased the volume of their singing. This was the era of much loss of life with the Port Isaac herring fleet, so the services were very poignant.

Both Richard and Sarah put into practice their Christian values, and young Bennett regularly walked down to the village, carefully carrying a cooked meal on a tray covered by a clean white cloth for someone who was bed-ridden.

Prayers and Bible readings were common-place in the Parson's home, and

THIS TABLE IS PLACED HERE BY MEMBERS OF THIS CHURCH AND CONGREGATION IN LOVING MEMORY OF
SARAH EDMONDS PARSONS
FOR 32 YEARS ORGANIST
AND A FAITHFUL WORKER WHO DIED AT SOUTHAMPTON ON JULY 2ND 1930, AGED 60.
"WHEN CHRIST WHO IS OUR LIFE, SHALL APPEAR. THEN SHALL YE ALSO APPEAR WITH HIM IN GLORY."

The plaque on the table placed in the Methodist Chapel in memory of Sarah Parsons. Courtesy of Richard Hoskin.

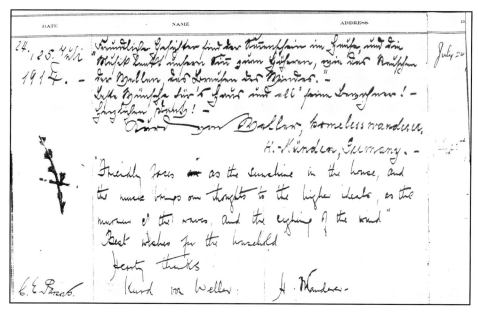

A photo of the guest book at 'Tredethlin' now 'Trethoway', Port Isaac, when the German spy who was staying there made this entry.
Courtesy of Richard Hoskin.

Richard was quite obsessive about protecting his children, believing that every aspect of his childrens' lives must be protected. Richard possessed a loud whistle, and every time the children went out to play, they needed to listen in case their father blew the whistle, whereupon they had to return home immediately. Also, it was no excuse for the children to say that they could not hear it, as that would mean they were too far away from home. Furthermore, the children could not lie to their father, and a cane hanging on the wall reminded them of the consequences. If the family went out walking near the cliffs, Richard tied his children together with a long rope as he believed their safety was his responsibility, and he never took chances.

As the children grew older, they were trusted to act sensibly, so they played on Port Isaac Beach like other children. They particularly liked watching the sailing vessels loading slate from the horse drawn wagons on Port Gaverne Beach. However, Richard retained his whistle, and the children were always alert for it. Occasionally there were even more exciting things for the children, such as when everyone dressed up for events such as Band of Hope Day, Empire Day and the usual fairs and parades, normally with a band, when the village came to life.

Once or twice a year the family made the journey to St Teath, to visit Richard's elderly parents who lived near the church. This was a long, bumpy, but exciting journey in a pony and trap. The lanes were uneven, and during cold weather the children snuggled down under the big blankets beside their parents, watching the flickering lantern outside, and listening to the rhythmic trotting of the animals' hooves. Richard and Sarah were always laden with goods and presents for Richard's parents, and the children looked forward to meeting their grandparents, with baby Bennett always immaculate in his Eton collar.

As the children grew older, Sarah taught Christiana how to play the piano, whilst Fred performed on the cello. Richard gave violin lessons to baby Bennett who was five, so there was much music-making in the house. The children all attended Port Isaac School, and they amused themselves playing with wooden sticks and hoops, and seeing who could push theirs the farthest. Walks in the country lanes were always popular with the family, and they picked fruit when in season for pies.

The children were very talented musically, and Richard and Bennett played on a Plymouth Radio Station. Richard and Sarah opened their home to visitors to help pay the bills, and young Christiana played the piano to entertain them.

By now, Frederick had passed for university, and Bennett needed more professional music tuition which Port Isaac could not provide. So between 1917 and 1930, Richard and Sarah moved to Southampton where the exceptional children prospered, another example of Port Isaac people having to move away to further their childrens' careers.

One day in 1930, whilst the family were living at Southampton, Bennett found a new canteen of cutlery in their house.

He said to Sarah, "What's this mother?"

Sarah said, "It's your wedding present for when you marry Mabel."

This was news to Bennett, and another example of the strict control Richard and Sarah held over their children. However, Bennett did marry Mabel on Boxing Day 1930, six months after Sarah's death by cancer, and Richard eventually returned to Camelford where he died in 1944.

Priscilla Milne, singing at Roscarrock Hill Chapel Sunday School, following the wedding of Edith Sweet and Richard Parsons.   *Julie Lowry nee Parsons.*   *Late 1950s.*

The Temperance Queen and attendants.
Back row from the left: Olive Welch nee Mortimore; Marion Wearne, Joan Bunt, Mavis Williams, Monica Welch, Ann Leverton, Stella Honey, Ruth Dinner and Eileen Hanson.
The girl standing in front of the back row is Edith Bate.
Front: Mark and Barbara Prout.
Courtesy of John Welch.   Early 1930s.

A photo taken at the time of the visit of the Rose Hill Methodist Youth Club from Derby, to the newly formed Port Isaac Methodist Youth Club. Harold Provis, the lay preacher and organiser of this event, sits to the left of the Minister in the front row.
Courtesy of Carol Brogan-Taylor nee Provis.   July 1949.

German Spy in Port Isaac in 1914.

In July 1914, a distinguished looking German gentlemen booked to stay with Richard and Sarah at Port Isaac for two days on the 24th and 25th, telling them he was on a walking holiday in Cornwall. He asked if he could have a room of his own where he could dine, and because he had heard Christiana play the piano when he arrived, he asked if she would play to him during the evening after he had eaten.

After that evening meal Christiana, then twenty three, went to move the table cloth, but the German asked her to leave it, as he wished to sit at the table while she played.

Christiana was a very accomplished musician, and could play most classical pieces without music, so she was able to observe the German in the polish of the piano. Each time she began playing he turned the cloth back, and began writing on paper hidden beneath it, and when Christiana stopped, he again pulled the cloth over his writing paper. During the following evening he did the same thing, so Christiana was now convinced he was an enemy agent. Richard was also now convinced of this, and he informed the local constable.

On the 14th August 1914, the spy was arrested near Padstow, just 10 days after war had been declared on Germany, and his name was Kurt Von Weller. He had written a touching entry in the visitors' book, pinning to it a sprig of white heather.

It is interesting that Christiana's musical ability led directly to the arrest of this German spy.

Methodist Youth Club.

Harold Provis, my uncle, organised the first youth club at the Methodist Chapel which was held after the 6 pm Sunday service. The photo is of the certificate confirming its existence, and it was held in the original chapel, the building which contained the chapel bell, and to the left of the main chapel. Later Harold moved to the Wesleyan Chapel and he started a youth club there. In fact it has been mentioned a few times, that Harold was mainly responsible for these youth clubs as well as organizing chapel outings.

The following are a few of the activities arranged by him for the Methodist Youth Club: A trip by train to Clapham, when the members saw 'the sights of London'; exchange visits with St Tudy Methodist Youth Club; entered a team in a six a-side football tournament at Tintagel; arranged a coach trip to see the wreck of HMS Warspite in South Cornwall; entered the Port Isaac

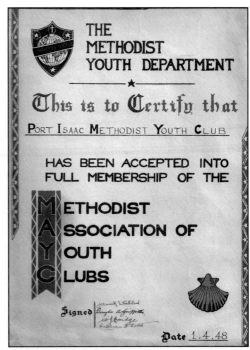

The original certificate of membership of the Methodist Youth Club at Port Isaac.
Courtesy of Harold Provis.

170

and Wadebridge carnivals with floats involving fishermen, and one float entitled 'Come back to Sorento'. In 1949 a Young Methodist Club from Derby also visited Port Isaac.

Harold also arranged trips to Gwennap Pit on Whit Mondays, and some of the chapel elders joined the youths on these occasions. He arranged for the high spirited boys such as Terry Gifford, Leonard Crockford and Bob Strout to go by taxi to keep them away from senior members such as 'Jennie' Hills. He told the boys that if they behaved they could go to Redruth Fair after the services.

Methodist Ladies Sewing Class/Annual Boxing Day Bazaar.

The chapel also boasted a sewing class, and these ladies made simple garments throughout the year such as aprons with material the group purchased for this purpose. This group included Mrs Susie Sherratt, Mrs Phillips, and Mrs Leonora Bate nee Smith, the mother of Steve Bate who was a good seamstress. Some of the poorer members paid a small amount each week to enable them to buy an apron, and on Boxing Day each year, a large bazaar was held in the Sunday School where a wide variety of goods were sold, and many people attended. Funds so raised went towards the chapel.

'Sunshine Corner'.

During the post Second World War years, a young Minister Mr Day, held community meetings in the Sunday School for the youngest members for two evenings a week, and this was named 'sunshine corner'. The children played games, sang songs, and generally enjoyed themselves, but with a religious 'bent'. Some senior members of the chapel assisted with this.

Methodist Chapel Teas.

There can be fewer better ways of bringing the community together than the chapel teas. These were held in the Sunday School, and were organised by the ladies. Chapel funds paid for the teas, and Susie Sherratt provided the food from her bakery during the first half of the twentieth century. This consisted of buttered brown and white bread, sponge and saffron cake which was sliced thinly and splits. The ladies provided the tea pots, and long tables were set out with white table cloths. The ladies waited on the members sat around the tables, and everything was served including the cups of tea.

These teas were served at chapel anniversaries, and on New Year's Day which consisted of a committee meeting at 2.30 pm, a service at 4pm and then the tea at 5 pm followed by another meeting or service at 7 pm. Stalwart ladies included 'Jennie' Hills, Mrs Ada Hills, Harry's wife; Mrs Arthur Hill, and Mrs Leonora Bate. Similar arrangements were made for Sunday school anniversaries, and a Minister always presided over the anniversary services.

Maurice Brown said that hens' eggs were collected at Whitsun on the Methodist Sunday school anniversary and put on a table beneath the gallery. Mrs Susie Sherratt was in charge of this which was a Second World War initiative. On the following Monday, the eggs were distributed to hospitals, mainly Bodmin Hospital, and this continued for many years after the war.

On Band of Hope days, chapel teas were provided as discussed previously.

A Roscarrock Hill Methodist tea in full swing. Alf Hooper is in the centre on the right. Probably taken during the centenary celebrations in 1969, hence the extra special arrangements.
Probably an Ellis print.
Courtesy of Grace Hooper and Barbara McKeown nee Hooper.

Another photo of the chapel tea at Roscarrock Hill. The Parsons family are at the rear, and Grace Hooper is in the centre on the right. Probably an Ellis print. Teas were a regular feature of the chapels, and helped forge their very good social function.
Courtesy of Grace Hooper and Barbara McKeown nee Hooper. 1969.

Methodist Praise and Prayer Meetings.

During the 1930s, on Tuesday evenings, 'Praise and Prayer' meetings were held in the Methodist Sunday School, and this was open to all members, young and old and many attended. These meetings enabled the members to get together, and socialise. This included hymn singing which the younger people enjoyed, solo performances, Bible readings, poetry and any item of suitable entertainment.

Methodist Womens' Fellowship.

These were a further example of the numerous social activities fostered by the chapels. This group met every other Tuesday at 2.30 pm in the Methodist Sunday School. Speakers on various subjects were the usual entertainment, and sometimes 'outings' by coach to various places were arranged. In 1966/67 the President was Mrs F Castle; Secretary Mrs RM Harris and Treasurer Mrs R Parsons. In 1986/87 the respective posts were held by Bertha Blake, Grace Hooper and Lilian Cloke.

World War Two Childrens' Guild.

The number of evacuees in Port Isaac during World War Two almost doubled the population of younger people. To assist socializing between the two groups a Childrens' Guild was organized. During these meetings stories were told by Mrs South, Mrs Hicks, Mrs Sweet, Miss Smythe and the Rev T Shaw. Team games were played between the evacuees and the Port Isaac children. (TS).

Methodist Choir.

The chapel boasted a choir which added to the communal singing. 'Jennie' Hills remembered going on a choir 'outing' to Newquay, and changing horses at Wadebridge and St Columb, this being an example of the effort the locals put into their social life.

Port Isaac Carols.

Port Isaac Methodists were justly proud of their congregational singing, including certain carols which were unique to Port Isaac. Sailors memorized tunes heard in distant ports, and applied these tunes to familiar carols, and others listened to ballad carols, and learned the parts by ear. However, this practice was not unique to Port Isaac, as many other places in Cornwall had their own carols and tunes. Indeed, Cornwall traditionally was a leader nationally in the singing of carols.

The initial performance of the world famous Service of Nine Lessons and Carols, was at Truro Cathedral during Bishop Benson's time.

Nicky Hicks and Julie Lowry nee Parsons, pictured at the Roscarrock Hill Chapel centenary celebrations in 1969. The cups they are holding were won for either singing or elocution.
Courtesy of Grace Hooper, Julie Lowry nee Parsons, Mary Mellor nee Hicks and Wendy Holland nee Hicks. 1969.

The Port Isaac Carol Service by candlelight at Roscarrock Hill Chapel was revived on the 12th December 2002 by Janet Townsend and George Steer, but recently this has again ceased. The following are a few examples of Port Isaac Carols:

Richard Hoskin's Grandmother Christiana Hoskin, 'Christine', wrote a pretty tune to 'Love Came Down at Christmas', words by Christina Rossetti. The tune is named 'Tregarthen', and is one of many written by her which were only sung at Roscarrock Hill Chapel. During the mid-fifties it was performed on the BBC radio in a Sunday morning religious service from Cardiff named 'Silver Linings'. It was not heard again after the chapel closed until the service was revived in 2002.

'Hark the Glad Sound' which has words written by Philip Doddridge (1702 – 1751), was also sung to a tune written down by Christiana Hoskin, who gave it to Mrs Tucker the organist. This is performed with different tunes elsewhere.

'Hark Hark' was traditionally sung outside of the Golden Lion Pub on Christmas Eve each year, and was written down from memory by George Steer, thereby ensuring its survival.

'How Beautiful Upon the Mountains' was known to the locals as 'Mountains'. Tradition states it was sung by the choir at Roscarrock Hill Chapel as the congregation left, but Richard Hoskin believes it was a Whitsun Carol.

So to sum up the subject of Port Isaac Carols; we had wonderful community singing in inspiring surroundings, with much of the musical content locally composed. To think that the chapel has been sold, in a similar manner to so many chapels in Cornwall, is surely a tragedy to any Christian of whatever denomination.

Walks after Evening Services.

During fine weather, some families made a point of walking around the country lanes surrounding Port Isaac. 'Jennie' Hills and her family walked either to Port Gaverne and Tregaverne, or up Trewetha Lane after the summer evening service; the absence of cars during the early part of the twentieth century making the walk pleasurable, and an occasion when families met for a general chat. I recall as a child regularly walking with my family up Trewetha Lane on Sunday afternoons during the 1950s, a more leisurely way of life than today.

A late photo taken during the service at the re-opening of the Roscarrock Hill Methodist Chapel at Port Isaac.
Courtesy of Pauline Stephens nee Brown. (Ray Bishop photo). 4th April 1981.

The re-opening of the Roscarrock Hill Methodist Chapel on 4th April 1981. From the left: Charles Symons and two Ministers. The minister on the left is Tom Darlington and the other the superintendent of the Camelford & Wadebridge Circuit. Courtesy of Grace Hooper and Barbara Mckeown nee Hooper. (Ray Bishop photo).

The Mitchell family regularly walked to Port Gaverne Main after the Services, all in their Sunday best, with the men wearing blue serge suits and the women often in black, with skirts almost sweeping the ground.

Circuit Youth Festival.

The Camelford and Wadebridge Methodist Circuit held an Annual Youth Festival in the spring of each year, in a town or village which had two Methodist chapels such as Port Isaac. This was necessary, so that one chapel was able to hold the musical events such as singing and piano playing, and the other chapel, the elocution events. During the mid to late 1960s, Roscarrock Hill Methodist Chapel enjoyed great success in this festival.

Adjudicating for a wide variety of handicrafts such as, knitting, sewing, woodwork, story and poetry writing, handwriting and photography took place before the day of the festival, and the items were displayed in one of the Sunday Schools. Other handicrafts such as painted eggs, model gardens and cookery were judged on the day. Points were awarded to each Sunday school for first, second and third places in all events, and these were added together, and a shield was presented to the Sunday school with the most marks. Roscarrock Hill's name was on that shield for several years in the mid and late 1960s.

One year, Barbara Hooper recalled the Port Isaac group dried up, whilst reciting an extract from the Pied Piper of Hamelin. They all stood just looking ahead, when suddenly they re-started the recitation, and the adjudicator remarked that this pause gave the verse real atmosphere, so he awarded them first prize.

The Cornish & Devon Post reported as follows: 'In May 1973, the 22nd annual youth festival was held at Roscarrock Hill Chapel. 270 children entered the various classes, and the number of entries was nearly 1,500. Twenty four Sunday schools were represented, and the handicrafts in the chapel showed a high degree of skill and originality'.

This is another example of real community work by the chapels, which has not been replaced following their demise.

Methodist Missionary Society.

Barbara Hooper recalls collecting regularly for this during the 1960s, and she entered the names of those who gave regularly into a small book. After one year of collecting, large medals and certificates were awarded to the collectors, and each following year, special circular badges were given and attached to the certificates, and a bar to go onto the medal. Dorothy Tucker of Port Isaac was such a Missionary, and she was abroad much of the time. Wendy Hicks recalls Dorothy talking to the chapel in the 1960s about her trips abroad.

Slide Shows at Roscarrock Hill.

Every week during summer, Grace and Alf Hooper put on a slide show in Roscarrock Hill Sunday School, of places to visit in Cornwall from Bude, then around the coast and finally finishing inland. This helped visitors plan their holiday, and it also raised money for charity and Grace always served refreshments after.

Local Girls Presented Services.

During the late 60s, a group of six Port Isaac girls presented Services in the Camelford and Wadebridge Methodist Circuits. They were Wendy Hicks, Janet and Linda Sherratt, Joy Harris and Pat and Barbara Hooper; although only four went at any one time. The girls divided the sermon, as well as different parts of the service into four parts, as they found that a different voice helped to keep the congregation attentive. Alf Hooper drove the girls, and dropped them off at a chapel, and he then drove to a nearby chapel where he preached, before finally picking the girls up and returning to home.

My maternal Grandmother Edith Mutton, a strict Methodist, left Port Isaac to find work at Plymouth, met and married a Catholic and consequently became a staunch Catholic, hence I am a Catholic also. However, many of my close family at Port Isaac were Methodists, and I have to admit to being very impressed indeed with the social aspect of their religion. I am very pleased that in 2013, there is much more religious tolerance in evidence.

Subscribers to Camelford Methodist Organ Fund 1909.

All the following were from Port Isaac unless stated:
Captain and Mrs Couch, Mark Guy, Port Gaverne; Mr TH Hills, Mrs E Hicks, Miss Martin, Captain W Mitchell and Mrs Mitchell; Mr S Prout, Mr & Mrs SN Stephens; Mr & Mrs Taylor, 'Craigmore'; Mr H Tom JP & Mrs Tom, Treharrock; Mr RE Tucker & Mrs GM Tucker, 'Homer Park'; Mrs Broad, Mr WH Symons, London; Mr H Symons, Wadebridge and Mr & Mrs Henry Symons Wadebridge.

This shows the close relationships enjoyed by the Methodists in various villages and towns.

The Wesleyan Chapel .

'The Chapel in the Valley'.

Sadly, the Wesley Chapel, formerly known as the 'chapel in the valley', was demolished about thirty to forty years ago. The large chapel and Sunday School were well named, as it was built in a wonderful setting in Port Isaac Valley, and many pictures of it were obtained from Church Hill.

A photo taken at Church Hill, showing the Wesleyan Chapel, known as 'The Chapel in the Valley'.
Courtesy of Pauline Stephens nee Brown.   C 1960.

The chapel is believed to have been the third on the site, which was once a skittle alley. Near to the steps of the Sunday School were bricks which once formed the entrance to the previous chapel on the same site. This chapel, the second, contained high backed pews, each with its own door, and the walls were white washed. The two sets of candelabra which hung from its ceiling, were transferred to the third and final chapel which was eventually knocked down.

The memorial stones for the new Sunday School were laid on 16th August 1874 by Miss Lever, Mr John Lever, Mr CW Provis of Manchester; and Mr HT Williams of Redruth. The Sunday School was opened on the 15th August 1875. Please note that three of the original four memorial stones have been incorporated into a wall remaining on the site, and as I write this I am very hopeful that at some stage, the fourth stone will re-join the other three.

The following is a copy of the poster applicable to the laying of the memorial stones to the Wesleyan Chapel Sunday School, Port Isaac.

'Wesleyan Sunday Schools Port Isaac.

On Sunday August 16th 1874, three sermons will be preached in the Wesleyan Chapel, Port Isaac. In the morning at half-past ten, and in the evening at six o'clock by the Rev John H Sholl of Manchester, and in the afternoon at half-past two by CW Provis Esq of Manchester. A collection will be made at the close of service.

On Monday 17th August 1874, four memorial stones of the new schools will be laid by Miss Lever of Manchester, John Lever Esq of Manchester, CW Provis Esq of Manchester, and HT Williams Esq of Redruth.

After which, addresses will be delivered by the Rev SW Christophers of Redruth, and the Rev CJ Preston, Superintendent of the circuit. The stones will be laid at three o'clock.

A tea meeting in the chapel at five o'clock, after which a public meeting will be

On the 17th August 1874, the four memorial stones of the new Wesleyan Sunday School at Port Isaac were laid by Miss KO Lever, Miss Ada lever, and Mr CW Provis of Manchester, formerly of Redruth and third from the left; and Mr HT Williams of Redruth. Four large slate stones with inscriptions were laid in the Sunday school wall, but the stone referring to Mr CW Provis was removed in good faith by the new owner of the chapel, and given to Mark, my late brother. Provis family photo. 1874.

held, chair to be taken by Ellis Lever Esq of Manchester.

The meeting will be addressed by Rev SW Christophers, John H Sholl, CJ Preston, Messrs Williams, Provis, Johnson, Symons and other gentlemen.

Tickets for the tea, one shilling each.

At the close of the meeting there will be a sale of useful and ornamental articles which were unsold at the bazaar held at Christmas last'.

I hope you appreciate the importance of these events to Port Isaac in 1874. I shall shortly give details of attendances of children at this Sunday school.

The following is a poster proclaiming the opening of this Sunday school, and please note the numbers of special guests who had travelled hundreds of miles for the celebrations.

'Port Isaac.
Opening of the New Wesleyan Sunday School, August 15th & 16th 1875.

'On Sunday August 15th 1875 at 9 am, the new schools will be opened by a Service of Praise and Prayer to be conducted by Mr Councillor Sinclair of Manchester.

At 11 am a Sermon will be preached in the chapel by the Rev JH Sholl of Manchester.

At 2.20 pm a Service will be held in the new school for children, parents and friends, to be conducted by Mr Councillor Collier of Manchester. A choice selection of hymns will be sung by the children.

At 6 pm a Sermon will be preached in the chapel by the Rev JH Sholl. At the same time and Evangelistic Service will be held in the school to be addressed by RF Farrer Esq; and four other gentlemen from Manchester.

This stone, laid by Mr CW Provis of Manchester, is one of the four memorial stones laid as described in the previous photo. This stone now remains with the Provis family, but we are hopeful that one day it may be returned to alongside the other three.

Photo by Geoff Provis.

The pulpit and Communion rail of the Wesleyan Chapel, Port Isaac, decorated for a harvest festival.
Courtesy of Clarinda Truscott nee Blake.

At 7.30 pm a Sermon will be preached on the Town Platt by CW Provis Esq of Manchester.
A Bazaar.

On Monday 16ᵗʰ August at 2 pm for the sale of useful and fancy articles will be held in the new school, and will be opened by Councillor Sinclair of Manchester.

At 3 pm a Sermon will be preached in the chapel by the Rev JH Sholl.

At 5 pm a public tea will be provided in the school room. Tickets to the Bazaar and tea, one shilling.

At 7 pm a public meeting will be held in the chapel, the chair to be taken by James Vickers Esq of Manchester, and addresses will be delivered by the Revs SW Christophers, JH Sholl, CJ Preston, and S Jones. Also CW Provis Esq of Manchester, Messrs Johnson, Symons and others.

NB. A collection at each service, (except the morning meeting, and the open air service), in aid of the new schools'.

Attendances at the Port Isaac Wesleyan Sunday School.

I have been very surprised whilst studying this, to discover the high attendances at this Sunday school many years ago, and also the degree of organization and effort put into it by the local Wesleyans. As an example I quote the constitution of the Sunday school on the 6ᵗʰ October 1895:

Superintendents – Thomas Johnson and Captain John H Dustow.

Boy's Bible Class – Mr W Martin. (Morning).

Boy's test Class – Mr T Mitchell. (Afternoon).

Boy's 1ˢᵗ Lesson – Mr F Gill. (Morning).

Boy's 2ⁿᵈ Lesson – Mr A Thomas. (Morning).

Girl's Vestry Class – Miss Symons. (Afternoon).

Girl's Bible Class – Miss Haynes and Smith. (Afternoon).

Girl's 1ˢᵗ Test – Miss Brown. (Morning).

Girl's 2ⁿᵈ test – Miss Morman. (Morning).

Girl's 1ˢᵗ Lesson – Mrs Burton. (Morning).

Girls 2ⁿᵈ Lesson – Miss Steer. (Morning).

On the following Sunday a different set of teachers presided, so they worked alternate Sundays. Also on occasions other people stepped in, so the effort put into the Sunday schools was considerable. The week after the above, the following were on duty:

Boy's Bible Class – Willie Symons. (Morning).

A Wesleyan Sunday school class photographed in the vicinity of the Wesley Chapel.
Front row from the left: Clarinda Truscott nee Blake, Michael Benz, Lloyd Polkinhorne, Martin Honey, John,
Jimmy and Edward Langton and David Philp.
Back Row left to right: Harold Provis, Charles Symons, Mrs Charles Symons, Phoebe Short, Mrs & Mrs
Cann of Middle Street, Pauline Brown, Mrs Stone and Mrs Williams.
Others include Ann and Amelia Philp, Jean Polkinghorne, Jennifer Honey, Michael Collings, Susan Benz,
Harry Morman and Jennifer Langton.
Courtesy of Carol Brogan-Taylor nee Provis.   C 1960.

Boy's Bible Class – John Edwards. (Afternoon).
Boy's 1st Lesson – Harry Morman. (Morning).
Boy's 2nd Lesson – Richard Morman. (Afternoon).
Girl's Vestry Class – Miss Symons. (Afternoon).
Girl's Bible Class – Annie Robins. (Afternoon).
Girl's 1st Test – Miss or Mrs Ernest Tucker and Miss K Smith. (Mng).
Girl's 2nd Test – Annie Remick. (Afternoon).
Girl's 1st Lesson – Mrs Burton. (Morning).
Girl's 2nd Lesson – Miss Steer. (Morning).

I do not have the attendances for the above two dates, but I am able to give you attendances on two Sundays in October 1899:

8th October 1899. Morning – 48. Afternoon – 64. Total = 112.
29th October 1899. Morning – 55. Afternoon – 71. Total = 126.

I find these figures astounding, and please remember these attendances are for Sunday school only. Many children also attended two Sunday services. Also at Port Isaac were the Methodist and Anglican Sunday schools, as well as Sunday schools at Trelights, St Endellion and Pendoggett. These facts alone must surely inform the reader of the loss of interest in religious worship during the last hundred years.

Sadly as time progressed attendances diminished, and I show you the following figures to confirm this:

April 26th 1914. Morning – 25. Afternoon – 38. Total – 63.

Sept 4th 1922. Morning – 12. Afternoon – 16. Total – 38.

In the space of just over twenty years attendances had shrunk remarkably, but dedicated Methodists and Wesleyans continued loyally to support their chapels although a more secular society was developing. I wonder about the effect of the First World War on religion and church attendances!

Over the years, numerous dedicated individuals have filled the roles of Sunday school superintendent, and in1929 Mr J Prout and Harry Morman filled this role. Sunday school teachers then included Mr JG Hawken, Mr H Spry, R Pink, Mrs Martin, Miss Inch, Mrs Jo Bate, Miss Richards, Miss Lark, Mrs W Couch, Mrs W Lobb and Mrs John Bate.

In 1963/64, Pauline Stephens nee Brown recalls that the total attending the Sunday school was about 18. Harold Provis taught the senior children from 10 to 14 years of age which numbered 12, and Pauline taught the under 10s which numbered about 6.

The New Wesleyan Chapel at Port Isaac.

For some time, local Wesleyans at Port Isaac had wished to replace the old chapel with a new one, and the following report in the Royal Cornwall Gazette of the 19th January 1883 gives details of some fund raising efforts:

'The Wesleyans of Port Isaac have for some time been desirous either to build a new chapel, or to renovate the old building so as to make it harmonize with modern tastes and requirements.

A bazaar was held with this object in view, and supplemented by a few friends it realized £65. 12s'.

The fund raising was obviously successful, so the chapel itself was opened on Good Friday, 3rd April 1885, and the following is a poster of the opening services:

'*Port Isaac New Wesleyan Chapel.*

Opening services.

On Good Friday April 3rd 1885.

A sermon will be preached in the above chapel by the Rev George C Mayes of Plymouth at 3 o'clock.

Tea will be provided in the School room at 5 o'clock, admission 1 shilling.

In the evening a public meeting will be held when addresses will be delivered by the Rev GC Mayes, the circuit Ministers, and other friends.

Chair to be taken at seven o'clock.

On Sunday April 5th two sermons will be preached by the Rev WS Gill, morning at 11, and evening at 6 o'clock.

A collection after each service for the building funds'.

It is worthy of note that the anniversary of this opening was celebrated at Easter each year at the chapel up until the date of its closing. This consisted of a special concert where members of the congregation displayed their talents in various ways,

Pauline Brown getting married to Colin Stephens at the now demolished Wesleyan Chapel, Port Isaac.
The minister in the picture is the Rev Jones, and Wesley Blake read the lesson and gave the address.
Courtesy of Pauline Stephens nee Brown.   2nd October 1971.

The Wesleyan Chapel at Port Isaac having been decorated for the imminent wedding of
Clarinda Blake and Keith Truscott.
Courtesy of Clarinda Truscott nee Blake.   19th April 1972.

either singing or playing an instrument. Following the concert, a special anniversary tea was enjoyed in the upper room of the chapel. Various chapel stalwarts ensured this tradition survived.

Mr CW Provis of Manchester again visited Port Isaac on the 5th and 6th August 1877, and I print details of the poster advertising his visit. My Great-Grandfather John Provis, a fisherman, gave him a row around the harbour in a small dinghy.

Port Isaac August 5th 1877

'Morning and evening. Two sermons will be preached in the Wesleyan Chapel by Mr CW Provis of Manchester in the afternoon at half past two.

An address will be delivered to the Sunday school and their friends.

No collections.

On Monday afternoon August 6th, a sermon will be preached by Mr Provis.

Service to commence at three o'clock, after which a tea meeting will be held in the school room. Tea on the tables at five o'clock.

In the evening at seven o'clock, a lecture on 'Home Sweet Home' will be delivered by Mr CW Provis.

Chair to be taken by Rev J Green.

Admission to the lecture 6d'.

Later in the twentieth century on Good Fridays, Mrs Pheobe Short accompanied the children to Pine Haven or Port Isaac Valley to pick primroses and violets to decorate the Cross. These flowers were again collected prior to Mothering Sunday in order that the children present the flowers to their parents. Again I must point out the community aspect of this, with the children walking over difficult terrain to collect primroses in the valley west of Port Isaac. This was also good for the children, and helped to teach them the value of service to others in life.

In 1956, an organ purchased from St Blazey was installed replacing an old French harmonium which had been in use for many years.

Easter Services.

On Good Friday, services were held with a bare Cross.

On Easter Saturday, the children decorated the Cross for the Sunday services, it being literally smothered with the primroses. John Cann, a local carpenter, made wooden ledges on which to put flowers as the windows of the chapel did not have sills.

Wesley Guild.

This was held on Wednesday evenings at the chapel, and consisted of Bible readings and talks in later years by such chapel lay preachers as Wesley Blake and Harold Provis. Various entertainments were provided such as slide shows, and on occasions Norman Reece sang with his deep bass voice. The meetings were very relaxed, giving the chapel goers an opportunity to mix socially. Usually about 18 to 20 people attended of various ages.

Sankey Singing.

Some chapels enjoyed singing Sankey hymns during special Sankey services, often held during the evenings. Port Isaac Wesley and Trelights Methodists enjoyed these events on occasions. Briefly Ira Sankey was one of a duo who wrote Christian songs which people enjoyed singing, and were designed to be inspirational to the congregation. The choruses were simple and repetitive, and evangelists such as Billy Graham used the rousing Sankey hymns to soften the audience before preaching. Sankey commenced his tours of the United States and the United Kingdom in 1871, and to this day, Sankey evenings or services are enjoyed by the surviving Methodists.

Wesleyan Fellowship.

This was started by Harold Provis in the 1960s, and consisted of Friday night Bible readings, the singing of hymns, and membership was open to all. Regular members included Ida Brown, Grace Hooper, Velma Knight and Shirley Coleman.

Port Isaac Odd Fellows.

The Port Isaac Branch of the Royal Camelford and Bottreaux Odd Fellows Lodge met at the Wesleyan Chapel Port Isaac, and the hall in which they met became known as Odd Fellows Hall. (See the section on 'lost societies' for full details of this organisation).

A scene from the wedding of Clarinda Blake and Keith Truscott at the Wesleyan Chapel, Port Isaac. The Port Isaac singers are performing the hymn, 'The King of Love my Shepherd is', and Josephine Provis, is singing the first verse as a solo. Josephine is on the left of the front row.

Rear row from the left: Joan Murray nee Honey, Anne Irons nee Julian, Merle Arnold nee Honey, Joan Orchard, Joyce Hambly nee Masters, Ida Brown and Pauline Brown. Partially hidden are Christine Saundry and Barbara Richards nee Finnemore.

Front row, Josephine Provis, Shirley Collings nee Gladwin, Elaine Found nee Short, Avis Wills, Jean Williams, Velma Knight nee Collings and Christine Hawkey nee Beare. The conductress is Janet Townsend.

Courtesy of Clarinda Truscott nee Blake.   19th April 1972.

1st Port Isaac Boys' Brigade Company.

For pictures of Port Isaac Boys' Brigade, please see the photos in the 'community celebrations' section.

Port Isaac Boys' Brigade met mostly at the Wesleyan Chapel in Odd Fellows Hall, and sometimes at the Methodist Chapel Sunday School and was first registered in 1937. The captain and chaplain then was the Rev HR Hewitt. It was closed in 1941, and re-started in 1942 when the captain was Mr JH Spry, (Harold Spry the coalman), and the chaplain, the Rev T Shaw. There was an average of twenty to twenty four boys, both evacuees and locals on the role, and in 1945 it finally closed. Jack Rowe said that Harold Spry was marvelous, and he kept the brigade together.

The brigade catered for boys aged eight, nine and ten. The uniform consisted of a cap, white shoulder bag and a belt. It is looked back on with much affection by local men who were members. Again, as with much in village life in days gone by, it was associated with religion, as it was in fact a chapel activity.

Its origins at Port Isaac are as follows: Alf Hooper, who spent much of his life at Port Isaac, originally came from Delabole, and he was involved with its introduction at Port Isaac. Alf, as a young man, was involved with the chapels at Delabole, and on one occasion a new Minister, the Rev J W Walker came to Delabole. He arranged a meeting, and he asked the young men if any of them had any experience of youth work. Alf said that he had three or four years with the Paignton Boys' Brigade so the Minister said, "Then that's what we'll have."

Apparently the vicar was thinking that after his three or four year stint at Delabole, Alf would continue the brigade. The Minister became captain of the Delabole Boys' Brigade, and it was really popular with every boy eligible to be a member. They met at the Sunday School of the Pengelly Chapel which is now closed.

Before long Boscastle, Camelford and Port Isaac also wanted to start a brigade, so Alf and some others visited these places, and so the Port Isaac Boys' Brigade commenced. Delabole Brigade visited Port Isaac on occasions, and they marched from the bottom of the village to the top and back again.

I asked Alf how the Boys' Brigade movement commenced.

He said, "My Uncle Smith in Scotland had a male Bible class, but when it came to the youngsters he didn't have a clue what to do with them. He realized with the men, that if he took a Bible class following drill parade he had their attention all the time. This was back in the 1800s, so he thought to himself, 'I wonder if this will work?' So he got as many boys together as were interested and he gave them the drill and the PT for about a half an hour, and then he took them to Bible class. He said they were all interested and they listened to all that was said. He called it the Boys' Brigade, so it started with the Church of Scotland. The motto was, 'The advancement of Christ's kingdom among boys, and the promotion of habits of obedience, reverence, discipline and self-respect, and all that tends towards a true Christian manliness."

Officially, William Alexander Smith founded the Boys' Brigade on the 4th October 1883.

At Port Isaac, Harold Spry the coalman conducted drill, Guy Hawken and Charles Symons of Trevathon Farm were leading Wesleyans and figureheads for the brigade. Young Bert Keat of Port Isaac, who was sadly killed in the Second World War, was a Sergeant of the brigade. During brigade meetings, the members were required to take part in Bible classes and drill, and they completed the St John Ambulance 1st aid course. Drill was practiced in the Odd Fellows Hall, and they marched at various carnivals. Harold Spry taught boxing and gymnastics, and Jack Rowe remembers giving a demonstration on the parallel bars. The brigade taught the boys to be smart and look after themselves. Most brigades finished with the outbreak of World War Two.

Wesleyan Youth Club.

Between 1942 and 1947, Margaret Larkin nee Castle ran the youth club. Sadly in 1949 she died, and a fire place was installed in her memory in the chapel room, because of her leadership 'around the fireside'. Ian and Noreen Honey were members plus George Steer.

Known as the Wesleyan Coffee Bar or Youth Club, this was very popular for a period, and was led in the early 1950s by Harold Provis, a lay preacher and chapel stalwart. It was held on Sunday nights in the Odd Fellows Hall after the 6pm to 7 pm service, and it gave the youth a chance to meet socially. They played cards, darts, pool, table tennis, and it had a coffee bar in the shape of a boat. I recall attending this club on occasions. Sometimes Charles Symons and his wife, stalwarts of the Wesley Chapel, looked in to see how things were progressing.

During the early 50s, a committee was formed from club members, and they organised several Port Isaac Carnivals. Mrs Hocking Lobb, and Mr Hillman, a Special Constable and local organiser, were co-opted onto the committee to assist, and working with Harold and the youth, they were indeed very successful.

Treviscoe Male Voice Choir.

In the account above of the Methodist Chapel, you will have read about the importance of community hymn singing at Port Isaac. This of course also applied to the Wesley Chapel, and before Sunday services for about a twenty minute period, the congregation were permitted to shout out the name of the hymns they wished to sing.

The visit of the Treviscoe Male Voice Choir from the St Austell area was always eagerly awaited by the local population. These visits were in February of most years, and they performed at 3 pm concerts in the Wesleyan Chapel. Following the service, trestle tables laden with food were put out in the Sunday School, and the chapel ladies served tea.

Recently I was talking to John Lugg at Delabole, and listening to him describe the current annual visits of the Holman Climax Male Voice Choir to the Methodist Chapel at Delabole. This reminded me of the local interest shown many years ago at Port Isaac, and the extent of the loss suffered at Port Isaac through the demise of the chapels.

An 'Outing' to Gwennap Pit, West Cornwall between 1948 and 1950.
Back row from the left: Yvonne Keat, Joyce Collins, Mrs Sweet, Marion Steer, Bob Strout, George Steer, Harold Provis,
Ian Honey, Noreen Brown, Frances Honey, ... Prout and Kate Townsend.
Next row: Thelma Stone, Henry Symons, Peter Rowe, Joe Saundry, Jean Sweet, Leonard Crockford, Barbara Honey,
Ivy Pearce, Maurice Brown, Brian Orchard, Mrs Brown.
Next row: Wesley Blake, John Cann, Morley Found, Elaine Short, Alison Short, Shirley Sloggett.
Front from the left: Tony Derbyshire, Tony Blake, Leonard Mapstone, Edith Sweet and Margaret Honey.
Courtesy of Peter Rowe.   C 1949.

Wesleyan Chapel Choir.

The chapel boasted its own choir, and they ably assisted the Treviscoe Choir during the 6 pm service.

Wesleyan Leaders Meetings.

Regular meetings of the chapel leaders were held until the very end of the chapel, and some records of these survive.

Lay Preachers.

As there were only three Ministers on the Camelford circuit, lay preachers were very important. When visiting lay preachers were used for a service, a car dropped them off at Port Isaac in time for the morning service, and then collected them after the evening service. A chapel member gave them a meal at lunch time. Port Isaac lay preachers also travelled to many other chapels, and during the Second World War, Charlie Lobb of the North Cornwall Garage, Port Isaac possessed the contract for conveying these. Tom Warne said that lay preachers who had preached at Pendoggett Chapel, regularly visited Tresungers Farm for lunch after the service. The business of lay preachers was important to the community, with so many active chapels in 'days gone by'.

A feature of the chapels was the number of ordinary folk who became lay preachers. Sammy Stephens, of Mitchell & Stephens Stores, Fore Street, Port Isaac was an early lay preacher, and others included Sam Blake, Alf Hooper, Wesley

Blake, Charlie Honey and Charles Symons. Warwick Richard Guy, a wealthy property and ship owner, was a Methodist lay preacher during the nineteenth century. My late Uncle Harold Provis was a dedicated lay preacher, and he knew Harry Morman, a local cobbler very well, he being a fellow lay preacher. Harry's small cobblers shop was in Church Hill, directly beneath my Great-Grandmother Ellen Mutton's house. Ellen regular complained to her family about the tapping of Harry's hammer as he repaired the shoes and boots of the village, as she tried to have an afternoon nap, but she never complained to Harry himself. Fifteen minutes was the advised time for lengths of sermons, but Harry's were usually rather long. Alf Hooper remembered preaching to over a hundred people in the Roscarrock Chapel before the Second World War. These lay preachers were dedicated men who travelled many miles in order to preach at the forty five chapels in their circuit.

Each circuit produced a plan, so lay preachers and ministers could plan ahead, however, ministers always presided over weddings, funerals and baptisms.

On one occasion, Harry told Harold of his duties on a particular Sunday: Sunday School – 10 am; Morning Service – 11 am; Sunday School – 2 pm, after which he walked to Port Quin to pray with Jimmy Martin; then to walk home to Port Isaac in time for the 6 pm Evening Service. Jimmy Martin worked two boats; the *Eclipse* and *Morning Star.*

Harry Morman, a Wesleyan local preacher for almost 70 years, and Sunday school superintendent for 50 years, was a gentle old man when I knew him, and Harold has composed this special poem as a tribute to his life and work:

Harry Morman's cottage in Dolphin Street. He grew his roses in the garden visible, but now this cottage and all but one cottage in Dolphin Street are holiday lets or 'holiday homes'. Many view this as progress, but it is progress at the expense of the local Cornish community.
Picture by Geoff Provis.   2013.

To Harry Morman, Lay Preacher.
A little man was WHM, and local preacher to,
And like Zacheaus who followed on, he followed his Master true,
He loved his chapel in the vale, he had his little pew,
Right in the back against the wall, and near the doorway too.
When ere he preached, he closed The Book, for notes he had no need,
And like the sower he went forth, to scatter Gospel Seed,
On the rostrum he stood firm, with voice so loud and clear,
And never faltered as he spoke, of his Great Master dear.

A Sunday night service on the Town Platt, with several chapel stalwarts present. Amongst those taking part are from the left: Charles Symons, Wesley Blake, Susie 'Gran' Sherratt, Mrs Charles Symons, Alfie Hooper, Richard Parsons, Barbara Hooper, Harold Provis, Gladys Stephens, Camelford; Keith Tucker, Annie and Jack Avery, Cyril and Ida Brown, Mrs John Stone and Dorothy Williams.
Courtesy of Grace Hooper and Barbara McKeown nee Hooper. C 1960.

He travelled around the circuit wide, and walked for many a mile,
In wind and rain and sunshine to, and always with a smile,
In Sunday - school for fifty years, he taught his little class,
And later on he 'Super' was, and never was surpassed.

He never faltered in his faith, when storms and sorrow came,
But proudly carried on his work, and never seeking fame
His prayers sometimes were little long, but his was a heart of gold,
And roses few he grew himself, were handed to the old.

How oft he travelled down Back Lane, with hymn book under arm,
Greeting the visitor as he walked, with grace and wit and charm,
He walked along the valley to, and learned from nature's lesson,
That God who loved the sparrow small, would ne'er withhold his Blessing.

For ritual he had no time, for him there was no need,
The Bible taught him all he knew, and Christ was Lord indeed,
His daily round was tapping shoes, in little cobblers shop,
Where passers-by, and boys and girls, paused and then did stop.

His heroes too were men of steel, like lifeboat crews the bravest,
And Billy Bray, revered by him, 'The Joyful News' his paper,
He walks no longer, Cornish lanes, he soles no boots and shoes,
But over in the Homeland, he sings his songs anew.

Harold Provis.

The paper 'Joyful News' is the Evangelical Newspaper published by 'Cliff College

I recall as a young boy the large roses growing outside of his cottage, and I also visited his cobblers' shop which was situated in Church Hill, and opposite the telephone kiosk. He was always willing to talk to us curious young boys, as we stood entranced by him repairing the footwear.

Clarinda Truscott nee Blake recalls being taught by Harry at Wesley Sunday school. She recalled that one saying from Harry has always remained with her. He told the class that before speaking to someone they should ask themselves, "Is it true, is it kind, is it necessary?"

Services on the Town Platt.

During the 1950s and 1960s, perhaps the most public feature of the work of the chapels at Port Isaac were the regular summer open air services held on the Town Platt after the evening chapel service. This location provided a natural theatre for the lay preachers and the congregational singing, and pedestrians could not help but hear the service. Regular preachers included Charles Symons, Harold Provis, Wesley Blake and Alfie Hooper. A small harmonium was regularly played by Grace Hooper or Charlie Honey.

Various other people sometimes led the service including those from Correstin Guest House on The Terrace, the home of Stan and Marjorie Bates; or next door at Rockmount, the home of Grace and Alfie Hooper. Visitors sometimes led the service, or people from Lowenna Manor at Rock.

This showed the chapel people to be very welcoming to other people, as well as a willingness to evangelise. I now look back with some admiration to those well intentioned people, and I believe that perhaps we are all worse off for the demise of such Christian activity.

Wesleyan 'Outings'.

Alf Hooper was nine when the First World War broke out. He said that they could not take holidays at Delabole during the war, so 'day outings' were arranged from Delabole to Port Isaac, using canvas covered wagons drawn by one horse. These 'outings' used the Polreworgey route into Port Isaac, as for a period near the beginning of the century, the Port Gaverne route was not available.

During 1923, twenty three Wesleyans contributed 1d per week towards an 'outing' to Rock which took place in July of that year. Prouts' buses of Port Isaac were regularly used for these 'outings'.

During the 1950s and 1960s, chapel 'outings' were an annual event, and St Ives, Falmouth, Newquay and Mevagissey were some of the destinations used. My Uncle Harold Provis organised many such 'outings'.

Wesleyan Stalwarts.

Pauline Duinker of Ontario informed me that her Great Grandfather Thomas Johnson, (1828-1897) helped found the last Wesley Chapel in Port Isaac. He was a Sunday school teacher and superintendent, steward and local preacher, and a memorial to him was erected in the chapel. This was taken to the Methodist Chapel when the Wesleyan Chapel was demolished. She recalled that on her visits to Port Isaac as a young girl, a Prouts' pony and trap took her and her family up Church Hill to visit the Symons family at Trevathon. The passengers walked up Church Hill, but Pauline remained in the trap. During my correspondence with Pauline, she expressed amazement at the demise of the chapels. She wrote, 'I thought there were many Methodists in the village, where will they go for services? I had no idea Port Isaac had become a ghost town. Where/why have all the people gone? I suppose there is no way left to earn a living except summer visitors'.

Willie and Charles Symons of Trevathon Farm, St Endellion were generous supporters of the chapel for many years. They were farmers, and perhaps a little better off financially than some others, and I often wondered what Charles thought when his beloved chapel was demolished. Other stalwarts included, Captain John H Dustow, Sam Prout, Guy Hawken, Harold Spry, Harry Morman, Harold Provis, Wesley Blake, Phoebe Short, John Prout, Charlie Honey and numerous other Sunday school teachers and helpers.

Both Wesleyan and Methodist stalwarts meet at the opening of the Wesley Room which was the newly refurbished cellar of the Methodist Sunday School building.
From the left: Dick Pooley, Ian Honey Maurice Brown, (Methodist); child unknown, Wesley Blake, (Wesleyan); John Sherratt, (Methodist); and Charlie Symons. (Wesleyan).
Courtesy of Grace Hooper and Barbara McKeown nee Hooper. C 1976.

Closure of the Wesley Chapel, the 'Chapel in the Valley'.

The nearest date I can establish for the closure is the mid-1970s. Money from the sale of the chapel was used to renovate the room beneath the Methodist Chapel Sunday School in Roscarrock Hill, and this became the 'Wesley Room'.

Whatever your faith, or even those of no faith, surely you cannot fail to recognize the importance to Port Isaac of its chapels. Sundays during my youth where characterized by the absence of work, and the sight of various families in their Sunday best making their way to their adopted chapel or indeed St Peter's Church. The three different bells rang out at various times, summoning the people to their places of worship. The very atmosphere of the village was one of peace, quiet and rest. The usual Sunday routine for the Wesleyan Chapel on Sundays during the 1950s and 1960s was; 11 am Service, 3 pm Sunday school, 6 pm evening service, and children were expected to attend all three.

It may be easy for non-believers to dismiss all this, especially in today's secular society, but this was the way of life of Port Isaac, and was even more so in previous days as I have explained above. It is true there were many locals who did not have any Faith, and there were many who did not approve of the Band of Hope, but the persistence of the believers against the rest, again helped to give the village its character.

Joan Dustow recalls as a young child living in Wesley House, Chapel Street, now Middle Street. Joan said that her mother Olive watched as Mrs Tucker from Homer Park Farm arrived for chapel wearing a black silk dress, and lots of beads which seemed to dangle over her dress. Her mother remarked how she was dressed better than most people. In fact, the area around the chapel was at one time a hive of activity throughout Sundays, and the people attending thought so much of their 'chapel in the valley'. Its importance to village life must not be underestimated.

Not every child wished to attend Sunday school, but it was an accepted part of village life, and parents usually ensured their child's attendance. My father told me that on one occasion he was attending Sunday school at the Methodist Chapel at Port Isaac, when he was so keen for time to 'be up', that he put a leg over the balcony onto the chapel clock, and moved the hour hand on with his foot, but unfortunately for him he was spotted.

John Wesley at Port Isaac.

John Wesley's influence on religion in the West Country including of course, Port Isaac, was massive, and the Methodist Church has always been justly proud of him. He was in fact a Church of England clergyman, but his preaching sowed the seeds of Methodism.

Following the turmoil of the Protestant Reformation, Christianity endured many years of uncertainty, and isolated towns and villages such as Port Isaac, provided Wesley with fertile ground to spread his message of the Gospel. He visited villages, towns and cities during the mid-eighteenth century, travelling on horseback, and his initial visits to such places often provoked a hostile response, but his persistence was quite remarkable, as he returned to such places time after time to deliver his message.

The following are extracts obtained from Wesley's own journal, and they relate only to the Port Isaac visits, but please be aware that he visited the whole of Cornwall, plus many other parts of England.

Saturday, 25th July, 1747.

'I was welcomed into Port Isaac by more company than I expected. The man who had sometime since headed the mob when they left Edward Greenfield for dead, had gathered all his troops, and received us as soon as we entered the first street. They all attended us to Mr Scantlebury's door, who (Mr T informed me), desired I should lodge at his house. I knocked long at the door, but no one answered. At length the master appeared – a hoary venerable old man.

I asked, "Pray, is Mr T here?"

He replied, "Mr T is not here, but pray, what may thy name be?"

I answered, "My name is John Wesley."

He replied, "I have heard of thee."

Perceiving that he had no more to say, I turned back to another house. The mob followed hallooing and shouting, but none of them offered to strike, or even throw anything. Only their captain, after some harsh words, lifted up his stick at me once or twice, but one of his companions interposed. He then quietly went away.

After spending an hour, we rode to Camelford. Threatened at Camelford and went to Tregeare'.

Author's Note: It has been handed down locally that Wesley was stoned by the villagers during the above visit to Port Isaac, but Wesley himself does not mention this. If indeed it is true, then Wesley clearly avoided mentioning such events, as in a similar vein, he avoids mentioning crowds showing huge affection for him later.

Wednesday, 19th September, 1748.

'To Camelford; thence to Port Isaac, and preached in the street at five to near the whole town, none speaking an unkind word. It rained most of the time, but I believe not five persons went away'.

Saturday, 25th August, 1750.

'In the evening I preached at Port Isaac in the street, the house not being able to contain the people'.

Thursday, 9th August, 1753.

'I rode to Port Isaac, and the next day at Trewalder'.

Wednesday, 31st August, 1757.

'Noon at Trewalder. Evening at Port Isaac. This was a long and barren soil, but is at length likely to bring forth much fruit'.

Sunday, 7th September, 1760.

'Trewalder. I then rode to Port Isaac Church, and had the satisfaction of hearing an excellent sermon. After service, I preached at a small distance from the church to a numerous congregation, and to a far more numerous one in the town at five in the afternoon. In examining this society, I found much reason to Bless God on their behalf. They diligently observe all the rules of the society with or without a preacher. They constantly attend the church and Sacrament, and meet together at the times appointed. The consequence is that thirty out of thirty five, their whole number continue to walk in the light of God's countenance'.

Tuesday, 21ˢᵗ September, 1762.

'Rode to Port Isaac. Here the stewards of the Eastern Circuit met. What a change is wrought in one year's time. That detestable practise of cheating the King is no more found in our societies, and alone that accursed thing has been put away, the work of God has everywhere increased. This society is particular has more than doubled, and they are all alive to God'.

Thursday, 5ᵗʰ September, 1765.

'Camelford Fair Day. I preached within at Port Isaac because of the rain, but many were constrained to stand without. It was a glorious opportunity; God showering his Blessings on many Souls'.

Monday, 15ᵗʰ September, 1766.

'Hence I rode to Port Isaac, now one of the liveliest places in Cornwall. The weather being uncertain, I preached near the house, but there was no rain while I preached, except the gracious rain which God sent on his inheritance. Here Mr Buckingham met me, who for fear of offending the Bishop, broke off all commerce with the Methodists. He had no sooner done this, than the Bishop rewarded him by turning him out of his Curacy, which had he continued to walk in Christian simplicity, he would probably had to this day'.

Saturday, 27ᵗʰ August, 1768.

'I went on to Port Isaac, now the liveliest place on the Circuit. I preached from a balcony in the middle of the town, a circumstance I could not but observe. Before I came to Port Isaac the first time, one Richard Scantlebury invited me to lodge at his house, but when I came, seeing a large mob at my heels, he fairly shut the door upon me; yet in this very house I now lodged, Richard Scantlerbury being gone to his fathers, and the present proprietor Richard Wood, counting it all a joy to receive a servant of God'.

21ˢᵗ August, 1770.

'Launceston, Camelford, Port Isaac, Cubert, St Agnes, Redruth and St Ives'.

21st September 1773.

'Cubert, Port Isaac, Camelford and Launceston'.

16ᵗʰ August, 1776.

'In the evening I preached at Mr Wood's Yard at Port Isaac, to most of the inhabitants of the town. The same spirit was here as at Camelford, and seemed to move upon every heart. We all had a good hope that the days of faintness and weariness are over, and that the work of God will revive and flourish'.

Monday, 28ᵗʰ August, 1780.

'I preached at Wadebridge and Port Isaac'.

Monday, 2ⁿᵈ September, 1782.

'I went on to Port Isaac'.

Monday, 29ᵗʰ August , 1785.

'Indian Queens. Port Isaac - dinner, letters, prayed, preached, supper, business and prayer'.

1789.

A 'footnote' to Wesley's visit to Cornwall in 1789; Watson writes: 'When he was last in the County, Wesley passed through the towns and villages as in a triumphal march, whilst in the windows were crowds of people anxious to get a sight of him, and to pronounce upon him their benedictions, yet he says not a word of it all'.

August 27th. 1789.

'Thence we hastened forward to Port Isaac. I preached in the evening in an open part of the town to almost all of the inhabitants of it. How changed since the last time when he that had invited me durst not take me in, for fear his house should be pulled down'.

Author's Conclusion.

The journal entries are an elegant testimony to Wesley's work at Port Isaac. He laid the foundation for over 200 years of Methodism at Port Isaac, and in so doing, made a huge contribution to the social and moral welfare of the community. Wesley's view of the attitude of society today towards religion would be very interesting, but I believe his main emotion would be one of disappointment.

Richard Wood of Port Isaac.

Little is written of Richard Wood, and there are no memorials or plaques to him, but he was very important to Methodism at Port Isaac. I refer you to the Wesley's journal entries dated 27th August 1768 and the 16th August 1776 and the references to him.

Mr W Symons writing on the 31st January 1951 wrote, 'There is one house in Port Isaac on the left as you go to "Wesley", where I've always understood John Wesley received much kindness from time to time. Some years ago a Captain Gill lived there for many years, and was proud to talk of Wesley's visits, so I've understood from my sister Mrs Harris."

Richard Wood was a shopkeeper in Port Isaac in 1765, and Harry Morman informed Harold Provis again in 1951, that a Mrs Fishley who died at Port Isaac in about 1900 was a Wood, and that she lived in or near the court in Middle Street, then Chapel Street.

I merely make brief mention of Richard Wood, as he was perhaps the most important person in Port Isaac Methodist history apart from Wesley himself. I have not studied him further as I attempt to confine my books to information I have obtained from local families and old newspapers.

Below is a brief portion of Richard Wood's Port Isaac family tree as obtained by Harold Provis, and I note that I indeed may be a relation by marriage via Richard Lobb.

Richard Wood married Elizabeth.

Children – George, Richard, Mary, Peggy and Elizabeth.

Elizabeth married Pasco Billing and they had the following children:

Elizabeth Billing who married Richard Lobb in 1836; Pasco Billing and Mary Billing.

Elizabeth, the widow of Richard, by her Will of 1812, left her 'houses and land' in Port Isaac to her daughter Mary. It appears that in 1831, Mary left her property to her nephew Pasco Billing Jnr and his two sisters, but I have not confirmed this.

Richard Wood, was a man of considerable interest and worthy of further study.

Acknowledgements.

I am indebted to the following people who have assisted me with my research, through either allowing me to use their old photos or information:

Anita Bunt nee Couch, Grace & Alf Hooper, Annie Price, Gerald Burnard, Peggy Philp nee Collings, Dennis Collings, Violet Richards, Bill Steer Jnr, Christine Glover, Janet Chadband nee May, Cynthia Hutz nee Stone, Warwick Provis, Warwick Provis Jnr, Ray Provis, Cyril Provis, Anthony Provis, Carol Brogan -Taylor nee Provis, Dorothy Oliver nee Lobb, Joan Murray nee Honey, Percy May, George May, Peter Mitchell, Arthur Mitchell, Nina Oliver nee Steer, David Hoskin, Richard Hoskin, Frank Rowe Jnr, Peter Rowe, Hermon Spry, Clarence Smith, Stanley Smith and Charlie Smith; Cyril Kinnings, Peter Castle, Henry Scorey, Eileen Jordan nee Bunt, Ann Irons nee Julian, Margaret Dingle nee Wherry, Melanie Dingle nee Wherry, Dennis Knight, Pauline Duinker, John Hawken, Stephen Found, Doreen De Mott, Priscilla Milne nee Hoskin, Annie Philp, Richard Couch, David Ham, David Hoskin, Peter Chapman, Susan Gettings nee Jones; Jimmy Langton, Michael Langton, Merle Arnold nee Honey; Marion Mewton, Barbara Richards nee Finnemore; Bernard Baker, Reuben Roseveare, Janet Townsend, Clarinda Truscott nee Blake, Maurice Brown, Cyril Spry, Michael Benz, David Bate, Ian Honey, Noreen Honey nee Brown; Bill Steer, Tony Gill, Brenda Burnard; Muriel Maling, Ida and Cyril Brown, Tony Gabriel, Pauline Stephens nee Brown; Billy 'Pom Pom' Brown Jnr; Juliet Cleave nee Tom; Terry Knight, Byron Buse, Phil & Debbie Tidy, Gwen Hooper, Olive Strout nee Honey, Wendy Holland nee Hicks, Graham and Kay Strout nee Byfield, Barbara & Billy Hawkins and Ann Smith.

Special thanks must go to Harold Provis, my late uncle and Wesleyan and Methodist Lay Preacher based at Port Isaac, for preserving some records and information; and to Richard Hoskin of Plymouth whose Hoskin, Billing and Parsons ancestors lived at Port Isaac. He willingly helped me with his encouragement and any request for information. Also, thanks to Barbara Mckeown nee Hooper, for making a special effort to supply me with more recent Methodist and social history, including many photographs taken during the 1950s and 1960s. Special thanks also to Bessie Selway for information about Port Gaverne and the Port Isaac Methodist Chapel. Special thanks to the Reverend Colin Short retired, of the Bible Christian Chapel who has willingly given me much information on the origins of Methodism at Trelights, including of course some fascinating details of the Trelights Bible Christian Chapel. Also special thanks to Joan Dustow, Jan Cowling and Roger Worth of Trelights. Special thanks to Joe Saundry, who allowed me much time to speak to him, and whose memory was very good indeed, and to Jack Rowe , Terry Gifford and John Welch.

Also, special thanks to Les Mitchell a Cornish Bard; Heather Mitchell nee Gladstone, June McCullam previously married to Harold Lobb; and Christine Treeby nee Lobb all of New Zealand, who have proved yet again that you cannot take the 'Cornishness' out of the Cornish. Christine was the 7th generation of Lobbs born at Hill Cottage, Rose Hill, Port Isaac.

Thanks to Plymouth Library for allowing me access to their newspaper archive, to the Truro County Museum Courtenay Library and the Cornish Studies library at Redruth. A few very early details of chapels I have obtained from the work of the RevThomas Shaw, and I have entered (TS) in the text where I have used this.

Finally, thanks again to Clive Benney of St Agnes for always being willing to offer advice, and to my long suffering wife Marlene for supporting me with this work and proof reading this book.

Geoff Provis.

Conclusion.

The object of this book is to explain the positive effect of Methodism on the social life of local isolated communities in the relatively recent past, and also the manner in which those communities socialised and enjoyed themselves, prior to the age of computers and mass travel. It is my contention that churches and chapels played a very positive role, and their continuing demise is a matter for regret.

Geoff Provis   2013.